Avoiding the CON in CONSTRUCTION

Avoiding the CON in CONSTRUCTION

*How to plan for hassle-free home building,
renovation, and repair*

Kia Ricchi

Centerline
Production

Centerline Production, Inc.

Published by
Centerline Production, Inc.
2425 McMichael Road
St. Cloud, FL 34771

Cataloging-in-Publication Data:
Ricchi, Kia
Avoiding the con in construction : how to plan for hassle-free home building, renovation, and repair
p. cm.
Includes index
Library of Congress Control Number: 2009908955
ISBN: 9780615310282

1.Contractors—Selection and appointment 2. Consumer education I. Title
TH4815.4   .R53   2010
692

Printed in the United States of America

Acknowledgement

Many thanks to my attorney, Mark Woodlock, who has worked
steadily with me for two years. His knowledge of construction law,
and his ability to explain it, has greatly enhanced this book.
He takes the complex and makes it simple and fun.
Long live the Lieniator.

To the reader

A construction project can be a challenging undertaking.
This book is intended to improve your odds of a successful outcome by
providing basic information about construction contracting topics.
But because every situation is unique, this information may not be
suitable for every circumstance. Therefore, please seek counsel with
professionals regarding matters specific to your project.

TABLE OF CONTENTS

The activities described
The cost of a flawed scope of work

Referrals: It takes one to know one
Contractors' work is a testament to their worth
Advertisements: Hear ye, hear ye
Content: Is it an editorial or an advertorial?
Internet advertising
Where not to look for contractors
Before you proceed
I spy, then verify

Professional licensing
Occupational licenses versus professional licenses
Occupational license: It's all business
Professional licensing: It's personal
Requirements for construction professional licensing
Knowledge
Experience
Financial and personal integrity
Continuing education
Verifying a contractor's professional licensing
Building Department
Professional Licensing Division
Inside the state website
Contractor licensing is for your protection

Protection against loss
Workers' compensation insurance
Why you should care
Building Department
Workers' Compensation Division
Authorized exemptions
Once again …

R-E-S-P-E-C-T
A quick look at inspections
From the bottom up
If the walls could talk …
The home stretch
Inspection=protection

Promises, promises
Liens and lienors
Foreclosure sales
Unfair?
Know thy lienors
Lienor's duties under lien law
Why weren't we introduced?
Owner's duties under lien law
Types of lien releases
Your safety net
(General) contractor's final payment affidavit
Unpaid lienors
Know thy lien laws
> *Lien Prevention Checklist*
The Lieniator says …

Avoiding the calm in complacency
Safety sleuths
Fall injuries
Excavation
Cranes and other hoisting equipment
Electrical hazards
Vehicle safety
Fatal Facts
Other matters that matter
Agree to disagree
Daily log
> *Work*

Preface

This book is a general introduction to construction contracting—a topic few home-owners know about, let alone understand—even though it can greatly impact their lives when they undertake a construction project.

Many homeowners think that construction is easy. They assume that when work needs to be done, they simply hire someone to do it while they sit back and relax. It's as simple as 1, 2, 3. This attitude may be the result of a past experience. Perhaps they saw a neighbor's porch built that was a quick affair once the lumber and carpenters arrived. Or maybe an addition was built that required heavy equipment such as cranes and loaders. To them, these exciting and impressive events seemed effortless. Seldom do they contemplate what takes place behind the scenes because construction is far more stimulating than the paperwork shuffle back at the office. Indeed, it is this excitement that may lead homeowners to rush into their own construction project without much forethought.

In contrast to those who are swept away in the moment, there are homeowners who recognize the importance of proper contracting but feel it is beyond their ability. Legal terms like "waivers of subrogation" and "aggregate limits" stop them dead in their tracks. Instead of seeking clarification of questionable issues, they submissively move forward with a contractor because they don't want to appear unknowing, suspicious, or rude. After all, surely the contractor is a professional who has the homeowner's best interest in mind.

Unfortunately, this is not always the case. The construction industry has a noticeable incidence of fraud and homeowners can be easily overwhelmed by the potpourri of laws, rules, and codes that regulate the construction industry. And the less that homeowners know, the more easily they can be misled.

Avoiding the Con in Construction

is written for homeowners in a language they can understand. It is for people who want an inside look at construction contracting so that they can make wise decisions when hiring contractors. This is what makes the book unique. It is a book about *how to contract*, not *how to construct*, and it is for the general reader, not the general contractor.

Did you know that:
   • Contracts are generally written to favor the author of the contract, that is,
     usually the contractor?

- Liens can cause you to lose your home?
- Without a clear and concise scope of work your construction costs could easily double?

A definitive scope of work is important because you won't reach your destination if you don't know where you are going. The assessment of licensing and insurance is equally important because it is the first step toward finding a qualified contractor. But even with a license in hand, how do you know the contractor is really qualified? This joke sums up the situation nicely:

What do you call the medical student who graduated last in his class?
Answer: *Doctor.*

Because the same is true of licensed contractors, you need to use additional methods to truly gauge their qualifications and character.

Avoiding the Con in Construction
also explains the permitting and inspection processes, and how they benefit you. Liens, jobsite injuries, and other costly events are also examined.

Whether you are planning a small repair, remodel or addition, or the construction of a new home, the same contracting procedures generally apply.

Undertaking a construction project can be an exciting process but it should also be a planned event performed with knowledge. At first glance, the broad subject of construction contracting may seem intimidating and, indeed, it is a challenge. But when broken down into individual topics, the information is more easily understood. This knowledge will help ensure that your project is completed correctly, on time, and on budget.

As my grandpa often said, "What you carry in your head is not heavy."

Cover Your Assets

Since man's early existence, shelter has been sought as a means of protection and comfort. Shelter from the weather, predatory animals, and fellow man prolonged survival. Today, in addition to providing shelter, homeownership is a symbol of independence and success. Our home, often the most expensive purchase we make during our lifetime, reflects our achievements.

Since the Great Depression, homeownership has risen steadily in the United States. The increase in homeownership may be partly the result of population growth and immigration. Homeownership may have also increased as a result of programs and initiatives created by the U.S. Department of Housing and Urban Development (HUD), banks, and other entities. Currently, the U.S. Census Bureau estimates that there are 130 million housing units (i.e., single family homes, apartments, manufactured homes, condominiums, etc.) in the United States.

But homes, like their owners, age. Homes should be maintained and repaired. Perhaps the water heater or air-conditioning unit must be replaced, or the roof needs new shingles. Other times a fresh coat of paint is needed to weatherproof the house. In addition to basic upkeep and repair, some people want to improve their home in more substantial ways and they undertake larger construction projects such as a kitchen or bath remodel or the construction of an addition.

Count on it: If you own a home, you will likely repair or renovate your home during your lifetime. And yet, often these projects—and they can be costly—are done without a thorough understanding of construction contracting. Because so few people understand the fine print of construction, this business is more susceptible to fraud than many other industries. In response to the harm that can occur from flawed construction and contracting, many states enacted laws to regulate contractors and their trade. But you must know the rules of the game in order to benefit from the protections they afford.

A project's success is often contingent on hiring a tiptop team of professionals who are experts in their fields. As with all professionals, the competency and integrity of contractors varies.

Fortunately, many contractors are upstanding, established residents in their communities. Some contractors own a family business that they plan to pass on to their children. Others work hard to create a profitable business that can be sold. These contractors recognize that good service at a fair price will enhance their likelihood of success because these attributes will attract and retain customers. A good reputation is essential to the long-term success of their companies.

But, as we all know, there are some bad apples who want to make a fast buck, and the tales of their wrongdoings are frequently aired on the news. This becomes particularly evident when a disaster occurs and a number of homes are damaged. Because of the abundance of work and the shortage of competent contractors, CONtractors arrive en masse to target desperate homeowners.

This was the case in 2004 when hurricanes Charley, Frances, Ivan, and Jeanne hit Florida. The National Oceanic and Atmospheric Administration (NOAA) estimated that Hurricane Charley's 100 mile-per-hour winds caused over $16 billion in damage. Even more devastating were hurricanes Andrew and Katrina, with combined damages exceeding $100 billion.

The television media aired footage of the fallen trees and power lines, flooded streets, and damaged homes, accompanied by emotional testimony from the victims. These homeowners were anxious for repairs so that rain, rodents, and vandals would not further damage their houses. Because of this urgency, many of these homeowners made poor contracting decisions, such as hiring the deadbeat who showed up with a pit bull and a promise. *Johnny Conman* promised to "git goin' in nothin' flat" once he received a cash deposit for materials. If the homeowners seemed reluctant, Johnny told them that it would be months until he, or anyone else for that matter, could get back to them. These scare tactics often convinced the owner to hand over a check without asking for Johnny's identification, professional license, insurance, or even a contract. Sometimes

Johnny Conman simply disappeared with the cash deposit. Other times, the repairs were worse than the damage itself. Either way, the owner experienced his own *Nightmare on Elm Street* in his *Little House of Horrors*.

Don't think that CONtractors wait around for disasters to make their move (and their money). CONtractors routinely rely on deception as a means of survival. Whether they tell a trivial fib or an extravagant lie, their goal is to get you to part with your money. Therefore, it is wise to heed the words of Sun Tzu in *The Art of War*, "Know thy enemy." By becoming familiar with a CONtractor's art of deception, you will recognize a con when you see one.

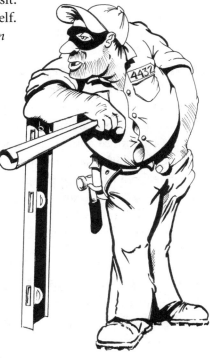

Heeeere's Johnny

CON 101: Introduction to CONtracting

It is well documented that deception occurs in business. CONtractors depend on dishonesty because their shortcomings prevent them from earning an honest living. Their trade is trickery and they have duped many unsuspecting homeowners by first gaining their confidence. The confidence trick, or con, is as old as time and it takes many forms. To avoid the con, you have to recognize it and the CONtractor behind it.

CON 102: Here today, con tomorrow

When a product or service is advertised, it is wise to consider both what is sold and how it's sold. Advertising is an effective means of marketing a product or service and it has a long history. In the past, town criers, or bellmen, were used to broadcast information. Using a handbell or horn to gain attention, they would communicate news about official matters such as war and laws. Criers would also make announcements about local goods and services. Today, people advertise their services and goods in phone books, newspapers, and magazines and on the radio, television, and Internet. Most contractors who invest in advertising are established residents with long-term commitments to their communities. In contrast, CONtractors have no allegiance to the community. They sell door to door because they do not have the credibility to set up shop. Without a business address, they rely on a cell phone number as their only means of contact. Beware of the CONtractor who shows up at your door because he may be a modern-day snake oil salesman—someone who promises quality goods but doesn't deliver.

CON 103: The story of Jack (of all trades)

Jack Tradesman is an expert storyteller with a gift for gab. Jack will tell you he's an expert who can "do it all." From grading, concrete, and framing to electric, plumbing, and mechanical, his accomplishments are broad and many. But is his story fact or fiction? There are indeed contractors who can perform a job from start to finish, especially if the project is relatively small. But a large project, such as an addition or even a substantial remodel, requires several specialty trades. A reputable contractor is honest about his abilities and will recommend other professionals to perform the work that is beyond his capability. On the other hand, Jack will attempt to do it all or perhaps subcontract some of the work to his pals. If Jack-of-all-trades is truly the expert he says he is, he must be able to prove it.

CON 104: For a low, low price of ...

In addition to exaggerating their abilities, many CONtractors claim that their price is a "great deal." But ask yourself, why are *you* being offered this great deal? Although many contractors are charitable, they typically donate their money or services to well-known charities such as Red Cross or Habitat for Humanity. Beware of the so-called "great" deal because it may simply be a means to lure you into a contract that won't be so great once you sign it. If the CONtractor insists on cash, this should also cause you concern.

CON 105: It's now or never

Disasters, such as a broken water pipe or house fire, can cause virtually anyone to make an emotional, illogical decision due to stress. CONtractors capitalize on this weakness and use pressure tactics to make a sale. Some CONtractors insist that if you don't "act now" you'll never find anyone to do the work because labor is in short supply. The elderly, some of whom may not be of clear mind, are especially susceptible to being misled and pressured into a sale that they do not fully understand, need, or want. Although materials and labor often are in short supply during and after a disaster, you are better served by hiring a reputable contractor even if it takes a little more time.

CON 106: You need more, more, more

CONtractors are experts at finding work that you need done. They seem to discover all sorts of problems that might threaten your health and well-being. Sometimes they justify these claims by citing building code violations. You should know that building officials, not contractors, issue notices of code violation. Additionally, older houses, although perhaps not compliant with current building codes, generally do not need to be modified in order to meet current codes unless they are found to be unsafe.

CON 107: Free money?

Some CONtractors claim that you will be reimbursed for the money you spend with them. Home improvement grants, offered by government agencies and private companies, are primarily made available to people with low incomes. Home improvement grant money may also be available to the general public who meet the requirements for the grant. For example, the State of Florida offered grant money to people who improved their home's resistance to hurricanes. This matching grant of up to $5,000 paid for improvements to windows, doors, and gable ends. States may also offer grant money to people who power their home with alternative energy sources such as solar or wind.

Beware of the CONtractor who promises that you will be reimbursed after the work is complete and he has been paid. Grant programs have strict requirements and you are only guaranteed the money once you are approved for the grant.

CON 108: The CONtractor shuffle

Licensing and insurance are topics that CONtractors want to avoid. When professional licensing and insurance is required of a trade, unlicensed CONtractors are forced to find a way around this significant obstacle. A common con is to claim to be "working under another contractor's license." States that require contractor licensing do not allow a licensed construction company to pull a permit for an unlicensed entity that has contracted directly with you. In Florida, this CONtractor can be punished for "deceitful representation and acting under a name not on the license." Insurance must also be held in the name of the company with whom you are contracting.

CON 109: Permit passover

Certain construction projects require permitting because the work, when incorrectly performed, can cause damage to you and the surrounding community. Through the permitting and inspection of construction work, the state ensures that trained professionals do the work to code.

CONtractors, who often do not have the license and insurance needed to pull a permit, may encourage you to pull the permit or to forgo the permitting process.

And the CON goes on

These are only a few of the many tricks a CONtractor will use to get you to part with your money. Cons are broad and diverse because desperation forces the CONtractor to be clever. But you can protect yourself by learning proper contracting methods. With an arsenal of knowledge, you will spot a con when you see one and steer clear of trouble.

Knowledge is power

Edmund Burke once wrote that "education is the cheap defense of nations." Education is also the cheap defense of individuals. With knowledge of proper contracting methods, you are armed to defend yourself against CONtractors who use deceptive tactics to get your money.

As with any business matter, the more knowledgeable you are about the business at hand, the better able you are to work with professionals and accomplish your goals. Therefore, not only do you have to find and hire professionals, you need to communicate and work with them effectively afterward. To be a contributing team player, you need to know the game, making you what is known in the construction industry as a sophisticated owner.

It's all about teamwork

Professionals rely on you to clearly define exactly what you want. Sure, they can offer suggestions, but the more thoroughly you define your goals, the more accurately and efficiently your work will be accomplished. While work is under way, it is also important that you, as a knowledgeable team player, help keep things on track. Mistakes can occur because large construction projects involve many people who perform a series of complicated tasks. These projects may require as many as 15 subcontractors on the job, each performing a number of distinct tasks to complete their work. Whether it is a minor scheduling conflict or a major discrepancy regarding material selection, you should play an active part in your project because you are often left to pay the price for the mistakes of others. Sometimes the project is delayed and other times the consequences are far worse. If you are a proactive member of the construction team, you are more likely to avoid costly mistakes.

It's in your hands

The construction of a new house (or repairs, remodeling, or additions to your existing home) should be a joyful experience as you watch your dreams become a reality. But if the process is plagued with delays and unexpected costs, it can be dreadful. Worse yet, you could land in court with devastating financial consequences. You choose. The outcome is in your hands. By learning proper contracting methods, as well as the laws that affect you when undertaking a construction project, you can proceed with confidence and wisdom.

Johnny B. Gone

The WHO, WHAT, and WHY of Contracting

Before the contracting process can begin, you must know the parties with whom you will be interacting. You must also understand the roles they play and the relationships they have with you and each other. The size of your job, as well as other factors, will determine whether you have a relationship with a few of these entities, or several of them.

The following people and entities often play major roles during a construction project:

The "who's who" of contracting

Contractor:
The term "contractor" is often used to describe *all* construction tradesmen—the general contractor as well as the subcontractors. When it is important to distinguish between the general contractor and the subcontractor, they are identified as such.

General contractor:
The general contractor, or GC, has the prime contract with the homeowner to perform the entire construction project. The general contractor's responsibilities are numerous and include estimating, contracting, scheduling, purchasing, supervision, etc. In the construction industry, the general contractor is also known as the prime contractor or prime.

Subcontractor:

The subcontractor, often called "sub" for short, performs a specialized construction trade such as plumbing, electric, framing, and so forth. These specialty contractors may also be called, for example, plumbing contractors or plumbers so as to better define their roles.

Sub-subcontractor:

Sometimes subcontractors hire other specialists to perform a portion of their contract. For example, an electrical subcontractor might subcontract the installation of an alarm system to a security company. This security company is a sub-subcontractor on the project.

Owner:

The owner, more specifically, the homeowner, is the person with a legal interest in the property.

Owner/builder:

An owner/builder is a homeowner who assumes the duties of the general contractor and contracts directly with subcontractors such as electricians and plumbers.

Design professional:

This individual is trained in the field of building design or engineering (or both) and may be a draftsman, architect, or engineer. Design professionals create the building plans and other construction documents needed for the construction project.

Building inspector:

This municipal officer is in charge of building code compliancy.

Construction lender:

The lender finances the construction project through "construction-perm" loans or other lines of credit.

Construction attorney:

Construction attorneys are often used to draft and review construction contracts. Unfortunately they are also called upon to remedy disputes between the contracting parties.

Supplier:

Suppliers are entities that provide materials and products to the construction project.

What exactly is construction contracting?

Construction contracting is the execution of construction contracts, followed by the management and fulfillment of the terms of the contracts. Depending on the nature of the construction project, the contract may be between the owner and a subcontractor—such as for a small home repair—or between the owner and the general contractor, which is often the case for larger more complicated projects. In this latter example, the general contractor and owner execute the **prime contract**, and the general contractor and his subcontractors and suppliers execute **subcontracts**.

The following graphic illustrates the chain of contracts between an owner, general contractor, and subcontractors. If the owner chooses to act as owner/builder, thereby assuming the duties of the general contractor, the owner would contract directly with the subcontractors.

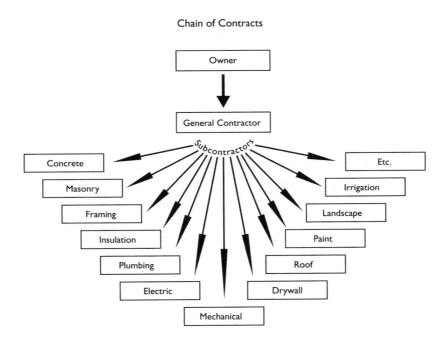

Chain of Contracts

The "why" of construction contracting

Construction is one of the oldest trades, as demonstrated by the existence of building remnants dating around 4000 B.C. in Mesopotamia. Mud brick remnants, made from local clay, were used to create buildings, temples, tombs, and protective wall fortifications.

The act of building permanent structures marked a transition from a nomadic lifestyle required of hunter/gatherer groups to the formation of stationary communities that relied on agriculture as their source of food. Whereas caves and temporary shelter had previously housed the nomadic tribes, agricultural societies built permanent and durable structures.

Many of these isolated communities developed into civilizations, characterized by a formalized political structure, the dependence on trade, and writing. As civilizations continued to emerge in Mesopotamia, other notable ancient civilizations formed in present-day Egypt, Pakistan, and China. The important role that builders played in the growth of civilization continues to this day.

Contractors provide a specialized service that requires them to:
- Interpret building plans to define the scope of work
- Quantify and estimate materials, labor, and their costs
- Find and verify the qualifications of potential subcontractors
- Solicit and review subcontractor proposals
- Draft and execute concise and inclusive contracts
- Obtain required permits for the job
- Order materials and schedule their delivery
- Schedule subcontractors
- Oversee construction and supervise subcontractors while on the jobsite
- Ensure jobsite safety
- Inspect the work for code and design compliancy
- Schedule and oversee building inspections
- Manage all financial transactions
- Stay current with laws that pertain to the construction industry

Although many capable homeowners assume the role of general contractor, others recognize that they fall short of the required knowledge, ability, and time required to successfully perform this role. Instead, they rely on experts to do the work required.

But one thing is for sure. Whether you act as owner/builder or hire a general contractor, it is essential that you, the owner, do play a role in your project because construction requires leadership and teamwork. Your role is important and it must be performed with care if your goal is to be reached in a timely and cost-effective manner. Without your meaningful participation, the outcome may fall short of what you desire.

PLAN THE WORK AND WORK THE PLAN

Construction is a series of events that requires well-coordinated teamwork by the team players, all of whom should have a clear understanding of the goal and the work needed to accomplish it.

As with any undertaking, planning improves your chances of success. When work is planned, it is focused and purposeful—and therefore more likely to be effective. When work is done without forethought, it is inefficient, wasting time and money. Failing to plan is planning to fail.

A successful plan should be concise, correct, complete, and clear. The most common complaints from homeowners who undertake construction projects are schedule and cost overruns. These problems arise when needed work is overlooked and, consequently, so are the time and money needed to accomplish this work. *Cost and schedule overruns occur when the game plan is ambiguous.* In construction, this game plan is the *scope of work*—the document that describes the project's objective and the construction activities that need to be performed. When a comprehensive and clear scope of work has been prepared, problems are less likely to occur.

The scoop on the scope

A scope of work is not exclusive to the construction industry. Many contracts describe the scope of work that will be performed in exchange for payment. For example, when you hire a housekeeper or landscaper, their duties must be clearly outlined. If you hire an attorney or consultant, their services must also be described. This scope of work is incorporated into the proposal they create for you, and subsequently, into their contracts.

The scope of work should also be well defined when you hire an architect, general contractor, or subcontractor. Will the architect only supply drawings or will the architect's fee also include site visits? Will the general contractor's fee include the cost of the permit and the building plans? This information, the scope of their work, defines the goal by detailing the specific activities that will be performed. If something is overlooked, that added service will typically cost an additional fee above what was originally negotiated. Because these additional costs can quickly become unaffordable, it is essential to list all of the work you require in your contractual agreements.

Although creating a scope of work for a construction project can be a challenging undertaking, you should do as much as possible given your knowledge of construction. Even if you have no construction experience, you can easily draft a scope of work for a small project. Larger projects, however, are more challenging and often require substantial construction knowledge. But any effort toward defining your scope of work is welcomed by the professionals with whom you will be working. For example, your scope of work will help the design professional create building plans that accurately reflect your vision. Additionally, contractors will be more able to correctly estimate and perform their work. Because the scope of work provides vital information, it helps to ensure that your project is done correctly, on time and on budget.

A sample scope—the Harris kitchen remodel

Although there is no standardized scope of work format or process for developing this document, the following example achieves the objective of a scope of work.

Project: Harris kitchen remodel.

Tasks:
Remove and replace kitchen cabinets
Remove and replace kitchen countertops
Remove and replace kitchen sink and faucet
Paint walls and ceiling

As you can see, a scope of work begins by defining the project objective and tasks in broad terms. As the scope of work continues to be developed, the steps, or *activities*, required to accomplish these tasks must be defined. Large jobs, such as the construction of a new house, will include some of the following building activities and associated elements.

EXAMPLE OF RESIDENTIAL CONSTRUCTION ACTIVITIES AND ELEMENTS

Jobsite preparation
Dumpsters
Portable toilets
Storage
Fencing
Electricity and water

Site
Surveying
Demolition
Clearing and scraping
Fill dirt
Rough grading
Compaction and testing
Chemical soil treatment
Fine grading
Final grading
Irrigation
Sod
Landscaping

Concrete
House slab
Garage slab
AC pad
Patio and porch slab
Sidewalks and driveways
Poured Walls

Masonry
Block, brick and all
precasts

Wood
Rough carpentry
  Framing (including trusses),
  decking, sheathing, etc.
Finish carpentry
  Trim, shelves, mantels,
  balustrades, etc.

Metals
Structural steel
Metal Framing

Electric
Fixtures
Fire alarms
Phone, Computer, TV,
  intercom, thermostat
Panel hookup to meter
  and street

Plumbing
Fixtures
Water heater
Septic system, lift station
Gas piping

Mechanical
(heat and air)
Grills
Dryer vent
Fans

Water and
weatherproofing
Roof
Gutters
Doors and hardware
Garage door and openers
Windows
Shutters
Insulation

Finishes
Stucco
Exterior Siding
Drywall including texture
Flooring
Paint and caulk

Wallpaper
Paneling
Tile walls
Murals

Specialties
Cabinets and counter tops
Ornamental steel including
  balustrades
Shelves, mirrors, partitions,
  accessories
Doorbell
Intercom
Security system
Lightning protection
Fireplace
Soffit
Screened patios
Fence
Flagpole
Address numbers and
  mailbox

Equipment
Refrigerator
Range
Dishwasher
Microwave
Garbage disposal
Garbage compactor
Washer and dryer

Special construction
Pool
Sauna and spa
Summer kitchen
Elevators and lifts

Miscellaneous
Cleaning

Smaller construction projects, such as the Harris kitchen remodel, are less complex and therefore have fewer activities. Notice that "cleaning" is listed as an activity. Cleaning is often overlooked although it may cost upward of $5,000 on a large project. ***Money also needs to be set aside for contingencies—those events that are not certain to occur.*** In this case, because drywall may be damaged when the existing cabinets are removed, money is put aside for drywall repair. If drywall repair is not needed, this time and cost will be a savings.

Construction Activities/Elements (Harris kitchen remodel)
Demolition (removal of existing cabinets, counter tops, sink, faucet)
Paint
Cabinetry
Countertop
Plumbing
General Clean

The activities described
Thoroughly describing each activity is an important step toward eliminating misunderstandings regarding needed work. As a rule of thumb, it is better to provide too much, rather than too little, information in the scope of work. Even cleanup is thoroughly defined as "removal of debris and broom swept." Additionally, each trade group is informed *where* this debris is to be placed. In this example it is in the dumpster. ***Only with a clear description of the work can a contractor correctly estimate and perform your work.***

Harris kitchen remodel: Activity description, further defined

LABOR AND MATERIAL LIST:

Demolition: Remove existing upper and lower cabinets, countertops, sink, and faucet to dumpster

Paint: Paint all kitchen walls Behr 854 Aztec Dawn Semi-gloss, 2 coats
Paint kitchen ceiling Behr 652 Florida White Semi-gloss, 2 coats.
Remove debris to dumpster and broom clean

Cabinetry: Measure and install upper and lower Kitchen Kraft Toscana Series Birch with knobs (see attached brochure)
Remove debris to dumpster and broom clean

Countertops: Measure and install Corian Prairie Trail with bullnose edging
Remove debris to dumpster and broom clean

Plumbing: Install Moen Chardonna #26884 sink – chrome finish
Install Moen Senore #90552 faucet – chrome finish
Remove debris to dumpster and broom clean

General clean: Remove any remaining debris to dumpster, broom clean.

Avoid ambiguous language when drafting the scope of work. Terms like "as needed" and "as required" are not definitive and allow for confusion. Instead, create a separate list of contingencies and their costs.

The cost of a flawed scope of work

The importance of developing a concise and inclusive scope of work cannot be overstated. The scope of work helps to ensure that an activity, and its cost, are not overlooked in the building plans and proposal, and consequently, in the contract. If an omitted activity is discovered after the contract is signed, a ***change order*** should be created and signed by the contracting parties. A change order is a written document that describes the added, deleted, or otherwise altered work and its cost or savings. (See example next page)

Since change orders typically increase the project cost, they are the curse of every homeowner. Most change orders result from:

- Errors and omissions in contracted work
- Work arising from unknown conditions
- Owner-requested additional work

Sometimes a change in work is initiated by other events. For example, an official from the municipal Building Department may require additional work that was not documented in the building plans.

Although an accurate scope of work will help reduce omitted work, it may not prevent necessary additional work due to ***unknown or hidden conditions***. For example, a site work contractor may be unaware of the large boulder beneath the ground until digging begins. A remodeling contractor may not know about termite damage inside a wall until demolition begins. If these conditions were unknown when the job was estimated, it is likely that their costs were not included in the contract price. Consequently, a change order is executed to allow for the change in the scope of work and contract price.

EXAMPLE OF A CHANGE ORDER

CHANGE ORDER

THIS ADDENDUM BETWEEN **New Home Production, Inc** AND **Kathleen and John Perry** SHALL BE INCORPORATED INTO CONTRACT # **PERRYKJ109** OF PROPERTY LOCATED AT **Pine Lake Unit 2 PB2 PG 9295 Lot 21 09 26-30**.

THE PURCHASER DESIRES THE SELLER TO INCLUDE IN THE DWELLING THE FOLLOWING OPTIONAL IMPROVEMENTS AT THE PRICES BELOW. SHOULD SELLER NOT INCLUDE THESE IMPROVEMENTS DESIRED BY PURCHASER, FOR WHATEVER REASON, PURCHASER'S EXCLUSIVE REMEDY SHALL BE THE REFUND OR CREDIT OF THE OPTION PRICE AND CHANGE ORDER FEE. THE SELLER RESERVES THE RIGHT TO DENY REQUESTS IN THE EVENT THE CONSTRUCTION SCHEDULE DOES NOT ALLOW FOR THE SAID CHANGE.

DATE OF CHANGE ORDER: **October 15, 2009**
DATE OF ORIGINAL CONTRACT: **January 3, 2009**

CHANGE ORDER NUMBER: **PERRYKJ109-12**

DESCRIPTION OF CHANGE: **Carpet upgrade in family room**
    PREVIOUS SELECTION: **Mohawk 7894-98 Burgundy Sunrise**
    NEW SELECTION: **Shaw 897-R Red Mist**

ORIGINAL CONTRACT VALUE: **$320,000.00**
SUM OF PREVIOUS CHANGE ORDERS: **$18,000.00**
CONTRACT VALUE PRIOR TO THIS CHANGE ORDER: **$338,000.00**
AMOUNT OF THIS CHANGE ORDER: **$1,985.00**
NEW CONTRACT VALUE: **$339,985.00**

CHANGE IN CONTRACT DURATION IN DAYS: **n/a**

PURCHASER: *Kathleen Perry John Perry*   DATE: **October 15, 2009**
CONTRACTOR: *Tom Builder*   DATE: **October 15, 2009**

Because change orders can be costly and disruptive, it is essential that the contractor include all needed work in the contract price. If you feel your construction knowledge is limited, consider asking an acquaintance who knows construction to assist you with the scope of work. If you think hidden conditions exist on your project, this person may also be able to help you investigate the matter at hand. Termite damage, for example, may be easily exposed by removing a small section of drywall or looking in the attic or the crawl space. Boulders are sometimes found by pushing a pointed metal rod into the soil. If you uncover hidden conditions, ask the contractor to include a price to correct these defects. This price may be stated as a time and materials charge if the contractor cannot determine the quantity of work he or she must perform. So do what you can to supply the contractor with complete information because the more information you give, the more likely the price will include all necessary work.

Because the change order document requires time to execute, many contractors charge a fee for this work.

Although change orders do occur in construction, they should be avoided; unexpected increased costs are always unpleasant affairs. Change orders may lead to a dispute between the contracting parties because often the owner is responsible for paying the additional costs associated with change orders. Matters can really escalate when a CONtractor greatly inflates the cost for this additional work. CONtractors recognize that they have the upper hand once the contract is signed and the job is under way because delays are troublesome. They know that homeowners want the job done promptly and that they will likely pay the additional cost to achieve this objective.

To help reduce change orders, develop a concise, correct, complete, and clear scope of work so that the building plans, proposals, and contract provide for all the necessary work. Once this is accomplished, stick to your plans and avoid change. Plan the work, and then work the plan.

Because hidden and unknown conditions are a possibility, you may want to set aside up to 10% of the contract amount for these expenses (i.e., contingencies).

CONtractor in paradise

FINDING THE RIGHT PERSON FOR THE JOB

It's official! Your construction journey is under way. But now that you know where you are going, who is coming along for the ride? Hiring a contractor is a serious matter because your goal—to have your job done correctly, at a fair price, and within a reasonable amount of time—is more likely realized if you have a top-notch workforce. These contractors are essential to the success of your project.

Finding this dream team is achieved by a series of small yet important steps. From assembling a broad pool of candidates to a thorough investigation of their qualifications, each step is a thoughtful process. Finding candidates should be done with care so that you chose people with the potential of fulfilling the requirements for your job. The following sources can be used to find these candidates.

Referrals: It takes one to know one

Referrals are highly valued because we would rather do business with someone we know, or know of, especially if this person has the positive endorsement of a friend or family member. But, as with any important business decision, it is prudent to apply strict standards.

When requesting referrals, consider the following question: Does the source of the referral have construction knowledge?

Ideally, the referral should come from someone who is knowledgeable about construction. For example, let's say that your friend recommends a carpenter to build your deck. Can your friend tell you what specific kind of carpenter this contractor is? A rough carpenter performs structural framing, decking, and sheathing, whereas a finish carpenter does more delicate work such as the installation of trim and casing. Because of the specialized training required for these fields, some carpenters are better suited than others to do certain work. Therefore, a rough carpenter may not be the right choice for installing crown molding in your home, and a finish carpenter may not be qualified to build your deck. When soliciting referrals, ask people who understand construction and make sure they have specific knowledge about the contractor's qualifications and past projects.

Are you working with an architect? Architects can provide a list of tried-and-true contractors because they are often called upon to inspect contractors' work. Additionally, because the architect is working for you, he or she shares your interest in getting your job done correctly, on time, and on budget. If you do not know an architect or other construction professional from whom to get referrals, consider visiting a construction jobsite.

 Always consider any personal motives behind a referral. Will the referral source benefit from the recommendation? Does he or she have your best interest in mind? Hiring a friend's son-in-law may not be wise if it leads to both a failed project and a failed friendship.

Contractors' work is a testament to their worth

When you want to speak to experts, sometimes you need to go to where they work. Many contractors are happy to share information about other contractors.

The benefit of a jobsite visit can be twofold. Not only does it allow you to speak with the experts, it may possibly allow you to visually assess their work. This look behind the scenes is an opportunity to judge the professionalism of the people working there. Is the worksite well organized and clean? Is the workmanship neat? Are the materials new? If you take a visual assessment of the workplace, you can confirm whether a contractor is indeed the professional he says he is. As a result, you may leave the jobsite with both a referral and a confirmation of its worth.

But be aware that your unscheduled visit may be disruptive and hazardous to you and those around you. Therefore, before you enter a jobsite, it is important to get permission from the general contractor or jobsite superintendent, who will escort you through the area. Once on the jobsite, stay with this person and be aware of the workers and their equipment. Electrical cords, tools, and building materials are trip hazards and may cause you to fall. Additionally, construction work can be dangerous, so be alert and cautious while on the jobsite.

Advertisements: Hear ye, hear ye

Contractors who advertise are good choices for your candidate pool because they demonstrate a desire to promote their business. This takes money! More importantly, it generally shows that they are committed to a long-term relationship with the community. If you plan to hire a contractor, it is best to hire one who will be around for a while.

Advertisements are a popular means for contractors to reach their audience: you. Many contractors place ads in newspapers, magazines, trade publications, and phone directories, both online and off. As a savvy consumer, you need to look beyond the printed word and ask yourself: Is the advertisement professional in appearance? Is the publication noteworthy?

Although an advertisement itself may not provide detailed information about a contractor, professional contractors generally advertise in well-known and respected publications.

Content: Is it an editorial or an advertorial?

Determining the professionalism of a publication can be challenging because things aren't often as they appear. Catchy photos and slogans can often distract from what should really matter: content. Good content focuses on the needs and interests of the reader, and should be newsworthy, comprehensive, and well researched. But, as with so many things, publications vary in bias and intent. While some publications are objective, informative, and have the readers' interest in mind, other publications strive only to meet their advertisers' needs.

An advertorial, in contrast to an editorial, has content that is influenced by the advertisers and therefore is less objective than a professionally written editorial. Because an advertorial is written to resemble an objective article, it can easily mislead the reader to believe that the information is unbiased when really it is only a cleverly disguised advertisement. In contrast, reputable publications are transparent and contain advertisements that are easily recognized as such.

Advertorials sometimes appear in magazines that are disguised as trade journals. These magazines, which at first glance may seem professional and objective, contain articles paid for by doctors, contractors, and others aiming to highlight their success. These publications are then given to clients as testimony to their accomplishments.

Use a keen eye to judge the newsworthiness of a publication before purchasing services (or products) listed therein. The featured contractor may have paid hundreds if not thousands of dollars for that article touting him as an "expert in his field."

Internet advertising

Because the Internet can reach a broad audience at a low cost, it has become an important medium for contractor advertising. A contractor's company website is a good source of information about his company's history, past projects, and future goals. In addition, the contractor's website should describe the services provided by his company and his area of expertise. Use these websites to determine whether the contractor might be a good match for you.

Online directories also provide another source of contractor advertising. Similar to a telephone directory, an online directory lists the contractors in the trade categories that best represent their services and products. Some directories, such as the *Blue Book of Building Construction* (www.thebluebook.com), ask contractors for their professional licensing (if their trade is licensed by the state) and will include the license number in the listing. Other websites play a more active role in matching you with a contractor. Bob Vila's website (www.bobvila.com) checks contractor licensing and works closely with the Better Business Bureau to ensure that its contractors are up to par. Service Magic (www.servicemagic.com) also helps to match contractors with homeowners and has an extensive contractor screening process in place. But be aware that some websites have lower standards, if any at all. These websites simply charge the contractor a fee to be listed and the higher the fee, the higher the contractor ranks on the website. Licensing may not be taken into consideration.

To ensure that you are dealing with a reputable contractor directory, research the website's contractor screening process, look for contractor license numbers within the listings, and review the website for overall professionalism. As was the case with the Wild Wild West, the World Wide Web requires you to arm yourself against the unlawful and inappropriate actions of your fellow man. Unfortunately, many innocent victims are harmed before the bad guy is caught.

Where *not* to look for contractors

Knowing where not to look for contractors is as important as knowing where to look for them.

CONtractors, like their fellow conmen, go where the action is, and there is lots of action at home improvement retail stores. These CONtractors may lurk both inside and outside the store. Because reputable contractors also frequent these stores, the CONtractor blends in perfectly until he walks up to ask you for work. Professional contractors do not hang out at retail stores and solicit business. They use more professional means of finding customers.

Before you proceed

Now that you have assembled a group of contractor candidates, you might assume that the next step is to contact them for proposals. Not so fast. You may want to review their qualifications first. Although some people contact contractors for proposals *before* reviewing their qualifications, this may not be prudent. Consider the following:

In order to get an accurate estimate of your project cost, you need to thoroughly review the scope of work with the contractor. To accomplish this, a close look at the building plans may be necessary, as well as a site visit to assess existing conditions. This review process takes a significant amount of time, which is wasted if the candidate is unqualified to perform the work. In addition, your safety should also be a consideration. If your project is a remodel, is it wise to invite a stranger into your home? Theft and other crimes can occur if a cleverly disguised CONtractor gains access to your house.

Although verifying a candidate's qualifications and character is time consuming, the process helps to ensure that the contractor is legitimate and worth consideration.

I spy, then verify

Researching a candidate's qualifications requires investigative know-how. You, as the lead investigator, need to know where to look and what to look for. You may be surprised by the abundance of personal information that is readily available to those who know where to look. Additionally, you may be surprised by the information you uncover. It was recently estimated that up to 50% of job applicants have discrepancies on their applications. Although many contractors are upstanding and honest individuals, CONtractors often lie about their qualifications. This deceit can range from verbal exaggerations to cleverly forged documents. Therefore, simply accepting a contractor's word and paperwork is not enough. If you want to make an informed choice, you are obligated to use due diligence. Fortunately, the Internet can help you to perform this research in a timely manner.

To find a contractor who is not only qualified, but also ethical, you need to look at both qualifications and character. Personal traits must be taken into account if you are to accurately predict how well the contractor will perform. A skilled contractor who can't keep himself out of trouble would be of no good use to you. He may be a real hot shot on the jobsite but that won't matter if he is in jail. Your job is on hold while he is being held. You need an expert with integrity—someone with a sound background who consistently demonstrates strong performance.

To assess a contractor's professional and personal standing, you should investigate:
- Licensing
- Insurance
- Public records
- Public reports
- References
- Professional memberships

The following chapters will guide you through the investigative process. This research can be sequenced as listed above and can be as extensive as you deem necessary. The higher your standards, the more thoroughly each candidate should be analyzed. Once your research is complete, a short list of at least three eligible finalists should be invited to submit a proposal for your review. With three or more proposals in hand, you should be able to find a contractor that best understands your needs and can perform the work at a reasonable price.

5
CONTRACTOR QUALIFICATIONS

Many states use licensing as a means to regulate an activity, particularly one that requires a high level of skill and is deemed dangerous when performed incorrectly. Take driving, for example. Driving requires skill and it is dangerous when done incorrectly. Therefore, licensing is used as a means to ensure that a level of competency is reached before a person is authorized to drive. Once this person demonstrates an understanding of driving and the ability to do so, a license is issued.

Professional licensing

There are many professions that must be performed with skill. Most professionals in the health-care industry are licensed because it helps to safeguard the public from the substandard performance of unqualified practitioners. A state may also require the licensing of professionals in law, finance, real estate, construction, and other occupations.

Contractor licensing, if required by the state, can help you gauge competency. So before you hire a contractor, it is important to verify his or her professional licensing. This is very important because the term "licensed, bonded, and insured" is used loosely in the construction industry. Here is an illustration of terminology used on numerous contractor advertisements and business cards.

27

Notice that Mike Smith does not clarify what types of licenses, bonds, and insurance he carries.

Research may reveal that Mike Smith does not have the often required:

- Professional license
- Licensing bond and/or
- Workers' compensation insurance/general liability insurance

It may, however, reveal a concealed weapons license, a bail bond, and life insurance.

There are many kinds of licenses and often a single professional will have several licenses, each with a specific purpose. The following will help clarify the difference between two well-known contractor licenses: an occupational license and a professional license.

Occupational licenses versus professional licenses

An occupational license is often mistaken for a professional license because the words "profession" and "occupation" are similar. The difference between them is this: *An occupational license pertains to a business while a professional license pertains to an individual.* Due to this common misunderstanding, some municipalities now use the term "certificate of use" or "business tax receipt" in place of occupational license.

Occupational license: It's all business

An occupational license allows a company to engage in business because it meets various governmental requirements for that occupation. Although each municipality has its own requirements, some common requisites for occupational licensure are:

- Fictitious name registration
- Registration with federal and state taxing authorities resulting in the issuance of a taxpayer identification number
- Professional licenses as required by the state

In addition, the municipality may require the business to demonstrate that it has sufficient parking for its customers and that it is compatible with the surrounding neighborhood.

It is important to note that ***an occupational license is not a professional license***. Whereas an occupational license authorizes a *company* to engage in business, it does not authorize an *individual* to perform a licensed trade.

Professional licensing: It's personal

Because professional licensing is typically required of people who can cause harm through the malpractice and misconduct of their trade, construction tradesmen are often licensed. Improper construction can cause catastrophic damage such as fire, flood, and collapse—and this damage may not be isolated to just one home; it may be widespread. Fire can devastate an entire community. Due to this potential for injury and death, many state governments enacted legislation aimed to improve both the quality of workmanship and the level of professionalism in the construction industry. This was accomplished through the implementation of building codes and licensing standards. Although the enactment of building codes has become somewhat uniform within the United States, regulation of construction contractors is somewhat less consistent.

Georgia, for example, only requires licensing for contractors in the four trades of building, plumbing, electric, and mechanical. In contrast, Florida requires the licensing of additional tradesmen—and California, still more.

Licensed Trades in the Construction Industry (2009)

Georgia
General Contractor
Air Conditioning Contractor
Electrical Contractor
Plumbing Contractor

Florida

General Contractor
Building Contractor
Residential Contractor
Sheet Metal Contractor
Roofing Contractor
Class A & B Air Conditioning Contractor
Air Conditioning Service Contractor
Mechanical Contractor Commercial Pool/Spa Contractor
Residential Pool/Spa Contractor
Swimming Pool/Spa Service Contractor
Plumbing Contractor
Underground Utility and Excavation Contractor
Residential Solar Water Heating Specialty Contractor
Solar Contractor
Specialty Structure Contractor
Pollutant Storage System Specialty Contractor
Gypsum Drywall Specialty Contractor
Gas Line Specialty Contractor
Internal Pollutant Storage Tank Lining Applicator Contractor
Precision Tank Tester Contractor
Specialty Glass and Glazing Contractor
Swimming Pool Specialties Contractor

California

General Building Contractor Insulation and Acoustical Contractor
Boiler, Hot Water Heating, and Steam Fitting Contractor
Framing and Rough Carpentry Contractor
Cabinet, Millwork, and Finish Carpentry Contractor
Low Voltage Systems Contractor
Concrete Contractor
Drywall Contractor
Electrical Contractor
Elevator Contractor
Earthwork and Paving Contractors
Fencing Contractor
Flooring and Floor Covering Contractors

Fire Protection Contractor
Glazing Contractor
Warm-Air Heating, Ventilating, and Air-Conditioning Contractor
Building Moving/Demolition Contractor
Ornamental Metal Contractor
Landscaping Contractor
Lock and Security Equipment Contractor
Masonry Contractor
Construction Zone Traffic Control Contractor
Parking and Highway Improvement Contractor
Painting and Decorating Contractor
Pipeline Contractor
Lathing and Plastering Contractor
Plumbing Contractor
Refrigeration Contractor
Roofing Contractor
Sanitation System Contractor
Sheet Metal Contractor
Electrical Sign Contractor
Solar Contractor
Manufactured Housing Contractor
Reinforcing Steel Contractor
Structural Steel Contractor
Swimming Pool Contractor
Ceramic and Mosaic Tile Contractor
Water Conditioning Contractor
Water Well Drilling Contractor
Welding Contractor
Limited Specialty
Asbestos Certification
Hazardous Substance Removal Certification

Because a state may develop a new category of licensing, you should check your state's Professional Licensing Division for current information.

Requirements for construction professional licensing

If a state determines that an occupation should be regulated through licensing, it must subsequently establish standards and requirements for the individuals seeking licensure. Applicants that wish to be licensed as contractors in Florida must be able to demonstrate that they are proficient and practiced in their trade and able to perform other duties that are required of them as professionals. Good character must also be demonstrated. Therefore, Florida and other states require the applicant to provide proof of:

- Sufficient trade knowledge
- Sufficient trade experience
- Financial stability
- A history free of dishonest and felonious acts

Knowledge

Testing has long been used as a means to determine a person's knowledge of a subject. Consequently, many states use testing as a means to gauge a contractor's competency. Florida, for example, requires an applicant pursuing a general contractor's license to pass a challenging test, administered over two days with nine-hour sessions each day, on the following subjects:

- Building codes
- Estimating
- Accounting
- Contracting
- Permitting
- Scheduling
- Energy efficiency
- Safety
- Law

In addition to this challenging test, Florida maintains a strict testing environment. The Florida Bureau of Education and Testing allows only approved books and materials to be used during the exam. Although these books may be highlighted and underlined, they may not contain handwritten notes or removable labels such as Post-it notes. Handwritten and typed notes in any form are prohibited, as are cameras, tape recorders, computers, and phones. Even hats and purses are off limits. Because of these strict measures, applicants must arrive early for a thorough screening and also provide photo identification before entering the exam area. Other states that require testing as a requisite of licensing may have standards that are less rigorous.

Experience

Because knowledge alone does not ensure competency, many states require a minimum level of work experience as a requisite of licensure. To demonstrate this experience, an applicant may be required to provide documentation of previous employment that describes what type of work was performed and when and where the work took place. This information is typically verified by the state for accuracy.

Financial and personal integrity

Before a contractor is entrusted with your money, he should demonstrate that he can manage his own. Therefore, states may require a credit report and financial statement in order to assess an applicant's financial history. A sound financial background most likely indicates that the applicant is responsible, reliable, and trustworthy. In addition, the licensing board may review public records for evidence of crimes that indicate a person's lack of moral integrity. Because fingerprints are considered positive identification, they are often used to check the background of people requesting licensure.

Since 1924, the FBI has been the national repository for fingerprints and related criminal history information. Today there are approximately 55 million criminal records. Statistics show that 12% of fingerprint background checks are linked to people with an existing criminal history.

Continuing education

Because new discoveries and innovations are continually developed, professionals must proactively stay informed in order to provide up-to-date services. As a result, many states require licensed professionals to continually educate themselves in their field and then show evidence of this education as a requirement of license renewal. Florida contractors are required to attend state-approved continuing education courses that address new developments in construction. Additionally, continuing education courses revisit issues that affect the construction industry on a continual basis. They include jobsite safety, workers' compensation, business practices, construction laws and rules, and building codes. Contractors who attend these courses are well informed on relevant issues.

When licensing is not required of a trade, a state may still require contractor registration. Proof of insurance and other requirements may be necessary.

Verifying a contractor's professional licensing

Because professional licensing is so important, it is essential to verify a contractor's license. But before you begin, you need to know your state's licensing requirements for the contractor's specific trade. Then you can check the contractor for compliance. Your state's Building Department and Professional Licensing Division can help you with this matter.

Building Department

The Building Department is the state's first line of defense against unlicensed and non-code–compliant construction because it enforces state laws at the local level. Through the implementation of a permitting and inspections program, the Building Department ensures that both the work and the workers meet the state's requirements. In order to obtain a building permit, contractors must not only demonstrate that the proposed work meets the state's building codes, but also that they meet the state's standards for contractors. To demonstrate that they meet the state's requirements for their occupation, they must often provide the Building Department evidence of licensing and insurance as a requisite of permitting.

Many Building Departments maintain a list of these compliant contractors. But be aware: This list may only contain the names of contractors who have pulled permits at that Building Department, rather than all the licensed contractors qualified to perform work in the state. *To obtain a complete and current listing of professionally licensed contractors, the state's list must be accessed.* Although the Building Department can assist you with your research, you can easily obtain this information online or by phone at your state's Professional Licensing Division.

Florida has both registered and certified contractors. Registered contractors have passed a local exam and can practice only in that locale. In contrast, certified contractors have passed a state exam and can practice throughout the entire state.

Professional Licensing Division

To ensure that professional licensing information is current and accurate, it is best to contact your state's Professional Licensing Division. This division provides up-to-date information about licensed occupations as well as the people licensed by the state. Although your state's Professional Licensing Division can be contacted by telephone, the Internet is a quicker means to access licensing information if you know how to effectively use an online search engine.

Search engines explore the web using programs that read websites and then index their contents. When you perform a search, your search words are matched against this index and the most relevant websites are then returned. Sponsored websites are highlighted and strategically placed on search engine return pages in exchange for a fee. For this reason, a sponsored link may not be relevant to your search.

The Internet allows easy access to a seemingly unlimited amount of information. The challenge lies in finding accurate, current, and complete information quickly. This is more likely accomplished if you enter the most relevant search words in your search engine. Since your goal is to reach a state website, the word "state" should be entered as a search word, as well as the state's name. Therefore the search words "state of Wyoming" should enable the search engine to return links to this state's website at the top of the page. Commercial websites that also contain content about Wyoming should be listed farther down the page. If you want the search engine to return links directly to this state's Professional Licensing Division, your search words should also include "professional licensing."

Appropriate search words are essential to a search engine's ability to provide you with relevant links. But before you proceed to use these links, they should be scrutinized for legitimacy. To ensure that the actual state website is reached, use links that contain the domains ".us" and ".gov." But note that some states, such as Florida and North Carolina, have website addresses that contain .com. Pay close attention to websites that have a .com domain because they may be privately owned, not state owned. For example, www.stateofflorida.com is a privately owned website and is not associated with the State of Florida whereas www.myflorida.com is the official Florida state website.

Contact information for all state Professional Licensing Divisions is contained in the appendix of this book.

Inside the state website

Although relevant search words are helpful in linking you with a state website, further navigation may be necessary once you arrive there. Many state websites also contain a search engine within the site to assist with this navigation. "Live chat," if available, allows you to instantly communicate online with a person who is familiar with the state divisions and their duties. Both of these helpful features can quickly connect you to the division that you seek.

EXAMPLE OF A GOOGLE SEARCH RESULT

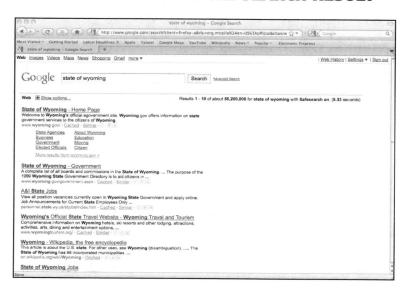

EXAMPLE OF A LICENSING WEBPAGE

Licensee Information

Name	RICHARDS, CHRISTY M (Primary Name) GREAT BUILDERS, INC (DBA Name)
Address	2466 Builders Rd. Anytown, FL 55583
County	Orange

License Type	Certified General Contractor
License Number	CGC078564
Status	Current, Active
Licensure Date	4/23/2005
Expires	8/31/2010

The website of the Professional Licensing Division (or similarly named division) should list all the occupations that the state regulates through licensing. Additionally, many state licensing websites contain a database of licensed (and previously licensed) professionals. In Florida, the Department of Business and Professional Regulation (DBPR) oversees professional licensing and maintains a database of licensed professionals, including contractors. This website also includes the names of those who have been disciplined by the DBPR. When using a database, read the directions closely because errors in punctuation, capitalization, and other factors may jeopardize the results.

The National Association of State Contractors Licensing Agencies (NASCLA) publishes a book titled Contractor's State Licensing Information Directory, *which contains each state's licensing classifications and requirements for contractors. Visit www.nascla.org or phone 623-587-9354 for more information.*

Contractor licensing is for your protection

Many states use professional licensing as a means to ensure that practitioners are competent and ethical before they are given permission to practice. As a rule, only knowledgeable and practiced professionals who demonstrate trustworthiness, honesty, and integrity are awarded a professional license.

Although each state implements its licensing programs differently, states share the goal of protecting you from harm that can befall you from unqualified practitioners. But the state can only do so much to protect you from these unlicensed and unqualified practitioners. You must defend yourself against loss by verifying the contractor's professional license—if one is required by the state.

In addition, you should ensure that the contractor is insured; licensing alone is not enough to protect you from harm. Jobsite injuries and other misfortune can occur, often resulting in loss. Because this loss can be devastating to you and others, many states require contractors to maintain various types of insurance. You must verify this insurance yourself.

Some states recognize other states' licensing requirements as equivalent to their own. Consequently they may allow reciprocity. Reciprocity, or the exchange of privileges, allows a licensed contractor in one state to forgo some or all of the licensing requirements in another state when applying for a license in the second state.

6
INSURED
AGAINST LOSS

Legal Disclaimer/Important notice to readers: The following overview of insurance is presented as general information only. It is not legal advice, that is, the application of law to an individual's specific circumstance. To be sure that you are adequately covered by insurance, consult with your insurance agent on a regular basis or have your policies reviewed by a competent attorney.

Risk is an uncertainty you assume every day of your life. Whether you are driving to work or building a house, the outcome of future events is unknown. Although your contracting experience will most likely be successful, there is always the possibility that loss will occur. Controlling this possibility by planning for potential loss is called risk management.

Protection against loss

Insurance is a resource that protects you against major financial loss because the risk of loss is transferred to the insurance company. In exchange for a small fee (the premium), you are protected against potentially large losses.

Loss can arise from many sources. Sometimes the loss is a direct result of an injury you incur. But you can also suffer loss if you injure another party. Take, for example, a car accident. You may injure yourself and another party. Because this loss can be substantial, most states require you to purchase automobile insurance as a requisite of registering a car. By mandating the purchase of insurance, the state ensures that you assume financial responsibly for the damage you may cause to others and yourself.

Businesses also engage in activities that can result in losses to themselves and others. Therefore state law often requires businesses to purchase certain types of insurance. For example, most states require businesses to purchase workers' compensation insurance as a means to protect company employees from the financial loss incurred from job-related injury, illness, or death. When workers' compensation coverage is not required, many businesses voluntarily purchase this insurance. A business may also purchase other types of insurance, including general liability insurance that may also be state required.

Workers' compensation insurance is compulsory in all states except Texas, which allows the parties to resolve their injury claims by arbitration, civil law, or other method. Although workers' compensation insurance may not be required by state law, many companies purchase this insurance voluntarily.

In construction, workers' compensation insurance and general liability insurance are essential not only to the contractor who purchases it, but also to the homeowner who may otherwise be exposed to loss associated with his or her project. Loss is often unjust. For example, if a construction worker is not covered by workers' compensation insurance and is injured on your jobsite, he may be unable to pay the medical expenses owed to the hospital and physician. As a result, these unpaid health-care providers and the injured worker may file a lawsuit against the general contractor, subcontractor, you, and others as a means to pay for costs associated with the injury. Lawsuits have been filed by members of the public who were injured while trespassing on jobsites. Regardless of whether these lawsuits have merit, all parties named in the suit must spend time and money to refute the claims. Because these losses can be substantial, it is important that insurance is in place and that you understand these types of insurances and what they cover.

A major difference between workers' compensation insurance and general liability insurance is that **workers' compensation covers the employees of a company while general liability covers the public affected by a company's operation**.

Workers' compensation insurance

The workplace has long been recognized as a site where injury can occur. This was most notable during the Industrial Revolution when new machinery, untrained workers, and long work hours contributed to the likelihood of an accident. Mines, textile mills, and foundries were particularly dangerous environments with high rates of injury. During the early days of industrialization, the law provided little compensation for the worker who was injured or killed at the workplace. Once the person accepted the job, he also accepted the responsibility for his own well-being. Business had little incentive to make the workplace safer.

But in 1911, the Triangle Shirtwaist Factory fire brought to light the need for change. When the fire started, many employees were unable to escape because the exit doors had been locked and the fire escapes were inadequate. As a result, more than 140 people died. Juries became more sympathetic to the workers' plight and awarded compensation for work-related injuries. This costly turn of events encouraged businesses to improve workplace conditions and expand workers' rights. Labor laws also evolved, and by 1948 all states had some form of workers' compensation laws in place.

Workers' compensation insurance covers the cost of medical, disability, and death claims of employees who suffer job-related injuries or illness. Workers' compensation also covers the costs of physical rehabilitation and vocational retraining needed to facilitate an employee's return to work. (These costs are subject to limits as provided by the laws of each state.)

Workers' compensation is often compared with no fault insurance because the employer's insurance company compensates the employee for an injury or illness "arising out of and in the course of employment"—even where the employee is partially or wholly at fault. However, such protection comes at a cost, as most workers' compensation statutes do not allow the employee to sue the employer for additional compensation or damages. This has become known as the great trade-off because workers' compensation insurance is generally the "exclusive remedy."

Each state has a unique workers' compensation program that is based in part on the nature of the work performed. Hazardous industries, such as mining, are more strictly regulated than the relatively safer retail industry. The construction industry also has strict policies because construction work is inherently dangerous. Construction workers perform labor-intensive tasks in dangerous environments. They use powerful tools while on ladders and scaffolding, and in areas where heavy equipment operates. As a result, not only does construction have a high occurrence of injury, but the cost to treat these injuries is expensive because the injuries are often severe and long lasting.

The Occupational Safety and Health Administration (OSHA) monitors workplace injury, illness, and death, and provides safety and health standards for the workplace. In 2007, OSHA recorded 5,703 occupational fatalities, 1,172 of which occurred in the construction industry (including extraction/excavation). The danger involved in construction is evident.

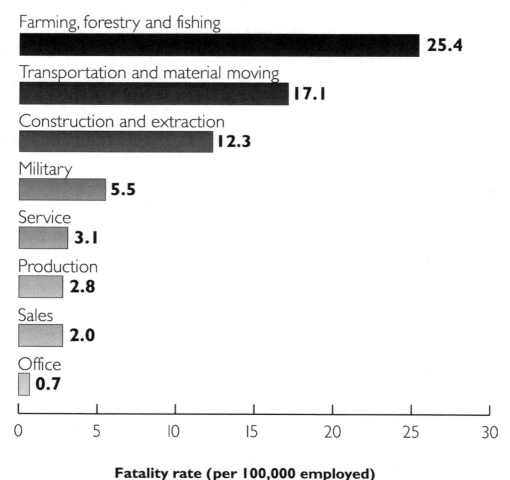

RATE OF FATAL OCCUPATIONAL INJURIES
BY SELECTED OCCUPATION GROUP, 2007

Farming, forestry and fishing — 25.4
Transportation and material moving — 17.1
Construction and extraction — 12.3
Military — 5.5
Service — 3.1
Production — 2.8
Sales — 2.0
Office — 0.7

Fatality rate (per 100,000 employed)

Source: U.S. Bureau of Labor Statistics, U.S. Department of Labor, 2009

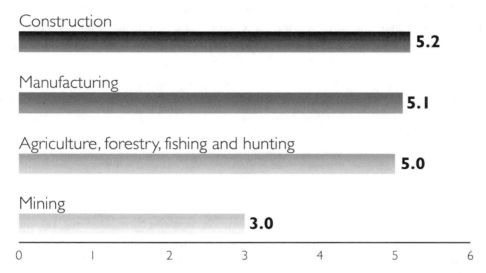

RATE OF NONFATAL OCCUPATIONAL INJURIES BY SELECTED INDUSTRIES, 2006–2007

Construction
5.2

Manufacturing
5.1

Agriculture, forestry, fishing and hunting
5.0

Mining
3.0

0   1   2   3   4   5   6

Incident rates per 100 full-time workers

Source: U.S. Bureau of Labor Statistics, U.S. Department of Labor, October 2008

Why you should care

When an uninsured construction worker is injured on a jobsite, sometimes he looks to others to cover his medical expenses. This may include you, which means you may incur legal costs in order to defend yourself. Therefore you should ensure that all workers are insured by workers' compensation insurance. A company's workers' compensation policy status, including any authorized exemptions, can be verified by your state's Workers' Compensation Division and possibly by your local Building Department.

Building Department

If contractor insurance is a requisite of permitting, the Building Department may be able to verify a contractor's workers' compensation coverage. But keep in mind that the Building Department may have information only on the contractors that have pulled permits at that department. Your state's Workers' Compensation Division can provide a more complete listing of insured contractors.

Workers' Compensation Division

Because the workers' compensation insurance program is overseen by the state, you should verify coverage directly with your state's Workers' Compensation Division. This ensures that the information is current and accurate. Many state's Workers' Compensation Division websites have a database that allows you to verify a company's policy. To navigate to this database using an online search engine, enter search words such as "workers' compensation" and "state of Florida," for example. Before you navigate to the links returned by the search engine, carefully review these links for web addresses that contain ".gov" and ".us" to help ensure that you reach the official state website. (Note that not all state website addresses contain these domains.) You can also contact the agency by phone. A list of state workers' compensation web addresses and phone numbers are provided in the appendix.

Authorized exemptions

Even though workers' compensation insurance is required by most states, provisions exist that allow exemption from coverage. A state may consider the number of employees, an employee's earnings, and the nature of the work performed when granting exemptions. For example, corporate officers may be eligible for exemption. These exemptions are generally documented by *authorized waivers*.

Although these authorized exemption waivers protect against claims of injury from the exempted individual, problems arise when this person, such as a contractor, brings a nonexempt (and uninsured) helper to the jobsite. If this helper gets hurt, he may seek compensation from his employer and anyone associated with the job—including you! Therefore, beware of the CONtractor who claims that his helpers are covered under his exemption waiver because workers' compensation exemption waivers are granted to individuals and not to entire companies. If a person is not covered by workers' compensation insurance or not legally exempt from this coverage, you may be asked to pay for injuries that occur on your jobsite.

In an effort to reduce the cost of workers' compensation insurance coverage, some companies run their employees through "leasing agents." In this instance, the policy covers specific individuals listed on the policy and not all the employees of the company. To make sure that a particular worker is covered, you must verify that his name is on the policy for the dates he is working on your project. As an added precaution, you should look at his driver's license to make sure that the name on the policy actually belongs to the person on your jobsite.

EXAMPLE OF A WORKERS' COMPENSATION DATABASE LISTING

Employer Information

Employer Name	GREAT BUILDERS, INC
Address	2466 Builders Rd.
City/St/Zip	Anytown, FL 55583
County	Orange
Employer Type	Corporation
NAICS code	561330

Coverage History

Effective	Cancel effective	Carrier Office	Policy Number
June 1, 2009	June 1, 2010	Anyone's Insurance Company	WC10896784
June 1, 2008	June 1, 2009	Anyone's Insurance Company	WC10896784
June 1, 2007	June 1, 2008	Anyone's Insurance Company	WC10896784
June 1, 2006	June 1, 2007	Anyone's Insurance Company	WC10896784
June 1, 2005	June 1, 2006	Anyone's Insurance Company	WC10896784

EXAMPLE OF A WORKERS' COMPENSATION EXEMPTION DATABASE LISTING

Exemption Details

Name	Title	Effective Date	Termination Date	Exemption Type	Employer Name
Anna Nichols	PR	May 24, 2008	May 24, 2010	Construction	Good Homes Inc.
Anna Nichols	PR	May 25, 2006	May 24, 2008	Construction	Good Homes Inc.
Anna Nichols	PR	May 25, 2004	May 25, 2006	Construction	Good Homes Inc.
Anna Nichols	PR	Jan 1, 2004	May 25, 2004	Construction	Good Homes Inc.

EXAMPLE OF A FLORIDA WORKERS' COMPENSATION EXEMPTION CERTIFICATE

04-04-2008

ALEX SINK
CHIEF FINANCIAL OFFICER

STATE OF FLORIDA
DEPARTMENT OF FINANCIAL SERVICES
DIVISION OF WORKERS' COMPENSATION

＊ ＊ CERTIFICATE OF ELECTION TO BE EXEMPT FROM FLORIDA WORKERS' COMPENSATION LAW ＊ ＊

CONSTRUCTION INDUSTRY EXEMPTION

This certifies that the individual listed below has elected to be exempt from Florida Workers' Compensation law.

EFFECTIVE DATE: 05/24/2008   EXPIRATION DATE: 05/24/2010

PERSON: NICHOLS   ANNA

FEIN: 59566677

BUSINESS NAME AND ADDRESS:

GOOD HOMES, INC
2687 WONDERFUL WAY
ANYTOWN   FL 55584

SCOPES OF BUSINESS OR TRADE:
1- CERTIFIED GENERAL CONTRACTOR

IMPORTANT: Pursuant to Chapter 440 . 05(14), F.S., an officer of a corporation who elects exemption from this chapter by filing a certificate of election under this section may not recover benefits or compensation under this chapter. Pursuant to Chapter 440.05(12), F.S., Certificates of election to be exempt... apply only within the scope of the business or trade listed on the notice of election to be exempt. Pursuant to Chapter 440.05(13), F.S., Notices of election to be exempt and certificates of election to be exempt shall be subject to revocation if, at any time after the filing of the notice or the issuance of the certificate, the person named on the notice or certificate no longer meets the requirements of this section for issuance of certificate. The department shall revoke a certificate at any time for failure of the person named on the certificate to meet the requirements of this section.

QUESTIONS? (850) 413-1609

DWC-252 CERTIFICATE OF ELECTION TO BE EXEMPT REVISED 09-06

PLEASE CUT OUT THE CARD BELOW AND RETAIN FOR FUTURE REFERENCE

STATE OF FLORIDA
DEPARTMENT OF FINANCIAL SERVICES
DIVISION OF WORKERS' COMPENSATION
CONSTRUCTION INDUSTRY
CERTIFICATE OF ELECTION TO BE EXEMPT FROM FLORIDA
WORKERS' COMPENSATION LAW

EFFECTIVE: 05/28/2008   EXPIRATION DATE: 05/28/2010

PERSON: ANNA NICHOLS

FEIN: 593503046

BUSINESS NAME AND ADDRESS:

GOOD HOMES, INC
2687 WONDERFUL WAY
ANYTOWN, FL 55584

SCOPE OF GENERAL OR TRADE:
1- CERTIFIED GENERAL CONTRACTOR

IMPORTANT

F Pursuant to Chapter 440.05(14), F.S., an officer of a corporation who
O elects exemption from this chapter by filing a certificate of election
L under this section may not recover benefits or compensation under this
D chapter.

H Pursuant to Chapter 440.05(12), F.S., Certificates of election to be
E exempt... apply only within the scope of the business or trade listed on
R the notice of election to be exempt.
E Pursuant to Chapter 440.05(13), F.S., Notices of election to be exempt
and certificates of election to be exempt shall be subject to revocation
if, at any time after the filing of the notice or the issuance of the
certificate, the person named on the notice or certificate no longer meets
the requirements of this section for issuance of a certificate. The
department shall revoke a certificate at any time for failure of the
person named on the certificate to meet the requirements of this
section.

QUESTIONS? (850) 413-1609

CUT HERE

＊ Carry bottom portion on the job, keep upper portion for your records.

DWC-252 CERTIFICATE OF ELECTION TO BE EXEMPT REVISED 09-06

Once again ...

When an accident occurs, there are often far-reaching consequences that are sometimes unjust. ***Therefore, in order to help protect yourself against financial loss resulting from an injury to an uninsured contractor working on your property, you must insist that all contractors have workers' compensation insurance or are legally exempt from coverage.*** If an exemption waiver is accepted, there must be strict orders that no other person is allowed to assist the exempt worker without having a proper exemption certificate or insurance.

General liability insurance

Whereas workers' compensation insurance covers the cost of an *employee's* job-related injury or illness, general liability insurance protects against claims from the *public* that result from a company's negligent acts or products. Additionally, although each policy differs in coverage, a typical general liability policy will cover property damage as well as bodily injury.

General liability insurance and property damage

During the course of a construction project, numerous contractors performing various trades build upon the work of the contractors before them. Whether attaching drywall to a framed wall or placing shingles on the decked roof, multiple tradesmen perform multiple tasks that result in the finished construction project.

Sometimes the faulty work of one contractor causes damage to the work of another contractor. For example, the roofer has the important task of installing a roof that is weather tight so that the house remains dry. If a roofing contractor installs the roof incorrectly and the roof leaks, this can damage the ceiling, walls, and floor. This damage to the work of other contractors is covered by the roofer's general liability policy. But it should be noted that this insurance does not pay for the cost to fix the defective roof itself. It only pays for the collateral damage caused by the defective roof. The cost to remedy the roof is the responsibility of the roofing contractor.

General liability coverage is an important safeguard against property damage because sometimes the damage that occurs during a construction project is catastrophic. Consider an electrician who improperly wires a house, causing it to catch fire while under construction. If this electrician does not have general liability insurance, and is unwilling or unable to cover the cost of damage, he may abandon the job leaving you to pay for the damage.

Insurance not only protects you from liability that might arise during construction; it can also protect against problems that arise after construction is complete. General liability insurance often contains a completed products clause that may protect against damages resulting from construction defects that arise after the building is completed and sold. Unfortunately, you may have no recourse if the contractor goes out of business.

General liability insurance and personal injury

Because personal injury claims are costly, it is important that you are protected from these costs, even those not associated with the contractors on your jobsite. Sometimes Joe Public is unintentionally injured (either on or off your jobsite) as a result of your project. For example, Joe may trip over your construction debris off the jobsite or he could fall in a trench on your jobsite. And surprisingly, some claims are made and won by people who trespass on a jobsite and are subsequently injured. These claimants may state that the jobsite was poorly marked and unsecured. The contractor's general liability insurance addresses the medical and disability expenses of these injured parties, thereby protecting you from costs that might be passed to you if the policy were not in place.

Verifying general liability policies

Because general liability coverage, in contrast to workers' compensation coverage, is not as strictly regulated by state law, state insurance divisions do not provide coverage information. Therefore you must ask the contractor to have his insurance company send the insurance certificate *directly to you.* This is a critical step toward assuring authenticity because forged certificates do exist. The Building Department may also be able to confirm a contractor's coverage if it has his or her paperwork on file.

Document consistency

Becoming a licensed and insured contractor can be challenging when a state's requirements are difficult and costly. Consequently, foul play may occur. Because insurance costs thousands of dollars, a CONtractor may submit a certificate of insurance with a name that does not match the name on the contract. For example, a certificate of insurance may be written to *Standard Services* while the contract is with *Standard Construction Services.* This may indicate that a CONtractor has paid another unscrupulous contractor to use his certificate of insurance.

EXAMPLE OF AN INSURANCE CERTIFICATE

ACORD®	CERTIFICATE OF LIABILITY INSURANCE		DATE (MM/DD/YYYY) 02/31/09

PRODUCER (555)555-5555 Contractor's Insurance Company P.O. Box 555 Anytown, FL 55555	THIS CERTIFICATE IS ISSUED AS A MATTER OF INFORMATION ONLY AND CONFERS NO RIGHTS UPON THE CERTIFICATE HOLDER. THIS CERTIFICATE DOES NOT AMEND, EXTEND OR ALTER THE COVERAGE AFFORDED BY THE POLICIES BELOW.	
	INSURERS AFFORDING COVERAGE	NAIC #
INSURED Great Builders, Inc 2466 Builders Rd. Anytown, FL 55583	INSURER A: Insurance Inc USA	
	INSURER B: United Employers Inc	10701
	INSURER C:	
	INSURER D:	
	INSURER E:	

COVERAGES

THE POLICIES OF INSURANCE LISTED BELOW HAVE BEEN ISSUED TO THE INSURED NAMED ABOVE FOR THE POLICY PERIOD INDICATED. NOTWITHSTANDING ANY REQUIREMENT, TERM OR CONDITION OF ANY CONTRACT OR OTHER DOCUMENT WITH RESPECT TO WHICH THIS CERTIFICATE MAY BE ISSUED OR MAY PERTAIN, THE INSURANCE AFFORDED BY THE POLICIES DESCRIBED HEREIN IS SUBJECT TO ALL THE TERMS, EXCLUSIONS AND CONDITIONS OF SUCH POLICIES. AGGREGATE LIMITS SHOWN MAY HAVE BEEN REDUCED BY PAID CLAIMS.

INSR LTR	ADD'L INSRD	TYPE OF INSURANCE	POLICY NUMBER	POLICY EFFECTIVE DATE (MM/DD/YYYY)	POLICY EXPIRATION DATE (MM/DD/YYYY)	LIMITS	
A		GENERAL LIABILITY [X] COMMERCIAL GENERAL LIABILITY CLAIMS MADE [X] OCCUR	08-MM-88776655	02/31/2009	02/31/2010	EACH OCCURRENCE	$ 1,000,000
						DAMAGE TO RENTED PREMISES (Ea occurrence)	$ 50,000
						MED EXP (Any one person)	$ Excluded
						PERSONAL & ADV INJURY	$ 1,000,000
		GEN'L AGGREGATE LIMIT APPLIES PER: POLICY PRO-JECT LOC				GENERAL AGGREGATE	$ 2,000,000
						PRODUCTS - COMP/OP AGG	$ 2,000,000
		AUTOMOBILE LIABILITY ANY AUTO ALL OWNED AUTOS SCHEDULED AUTOS HIRED AUTOS NON-OWNED AUTOS				COMBINED SINGLE LIMIT (Ea accident)	$
						BODILY INJURY (Per person)	$
						BODILY INJURY (Per accident)	$
						PROPERTY DAMAGE (Per accident)	$
		GARAGE LIABILITY ANY AUTO				AUTO ONLY - EA ACCIDENT	$
						OTHER THAN AUTO ONLY: EA ACC	$
						AGG	$
		EXCESS / UMBRELLA LIABILITY OCCUR CLAIMS MADE				EACH OCCURRENCE	$
						AGGREGATE	$
		DEDUCTIBLE RETENTION $					$
							$
B		WORKERS COMPENSATION AND EMPLOYERS' LIABILITY ANY PROPRIETOR/PARTNER/EXECUTIVE OFFICER/MEMBER EXCLUDED? (Mandatory in NH) If yes, describe under SPECIAL PROVISIONS below	123456789	02/31/2009	02/31/2010	[X] WC STATU-TORY LIMITS OTH-ER	
		Y/N [N]				E.L. EACH ACCIDENT	$ 100,000
						E.L. DISEASE - EA EMPLOYEE	$ 100,000
		OTHER				E.L. DISEASE - POLICY LIMIT	$ 500,000

DESCRIPTION OF OPERATIONS / LOCATIONS / VEHICLES / EXCLUSIONS ADDED BY ENDORSEMENT / SPECIAL PROVISIONS

CERTIFICATE HOLDER	CANCELLATION
Henry Homeowner 7777 Main St. Anytown, FL 55584	SHOULD ANY OF THE ABOVE DESCRIBED POLICIES BE CANCELLED BEFORE THE EXPIRATION DATE THEREOF, THE ISSUING INSURER WILL ENDEAVOR TO MAIL __10__ DAYS WRITTEN NOTICE TO THE CERTIFICATE HOLDER NAMED TO THE LEFT, BUT FAILURE TO DO SO SHALL IMPOSE NO OBLIGATION OR LIABILITY OF ANY KIND UPON THE INSURER, ITS AGENTS OR REPRESENTATIVES.
	AUTHORIZED REPRESENTATIVE Alan Agent

ACORD 25 (2009/01)   © 1988-2009 ACORD CORPORATION. All rights reserved.

The ACORD name and logo are registered marks of ACORD

If there are inconsistencies with the license, insurance, and contract documents, you may be dealing with a CONtractor.

Additional protection

In order to create a stronger defense against claims, you can ask to be listed as either a **certificate holder** or **additional insured** on the contractor's insurance policy. The distinction between a certificate holder and an additional insured is important. As a certificate holder, you are informed of any changes in the contractor's policy, such as policy amounts, cancellations, and renewals. This is a valuable service, particularly if the contractor's policy is cancelled.

Just as the term suggests, when you are listed as additional insured, you are added to the contractor's policy. As a result, if a claim or suit is filed that is covered by the policy and you are named in the suit, the insurance company will likely defend you and pay your legal fees if the contractor is at fault. If you are not listed as additional insured, you must pay for your own legal defense. Although there is a fee to be listed as additional insured, you may find it beneficial to be listed on the general contractor's policy, as well as all subcontractors' policies.

Policy limits

In addition to confirming that a company is insured, it is equally important to review the amount of coverage the contractor has purchased because if the coverage is insufficient to cover a claim, you may be responsible for paying the remaining amounts should a lawsuit be filed. Although some states specify a contractor's minimum amount of general liability coverage at $300,000, your insurance agent may recommend minimum coverage of between $500,000 and $1,000,000. To determine whether you are adequately protected by a contractor's policy, meet with your insurance agent.

Builders' risk insurance

Many people are familiar with homeowners' insurance as a means to protect the finished home from damage arising from fire, theft, and other losses. In contrast, sometimes the value of the house is overlooked while it is under construction. From the moment your project breaks ground, thousands of dollars are spent to complete it. While under construction, your project is also exposed to the damages of fire, flood, windstorms, vandalism, and other perils. For example, trusses and block walls can fall over as a result of strong winds. Therefore, a new house, as well as any costly renovations and additions, should be insured while construction is under way.

Builders' risk insurance is a form of property insurance that protects against the loss of material and labor costs while the house is under construction. In addition to insuring the materials and labor already incorporated into the building, builders' risk insurance covers the cost of materials stored on site that are damaged or lost due to most "Acts of God." A separate policy rider typically covers loss due to theft.

Whereas workers' compensation and general liability insurance are often required by the state, builders' risk insurance is not. Instead, your lender may require evidence of builders' risk insurance if your project is financed by a construction loan. If a line of credit is used, builders' risk insurance may not be required. Nevertheless, builders' risk insurance is a vital source of protection against financial loss and is available for new construction as well as for remodels and additions. When reviewing a policy, be mindful of any exclusions, such as those related to damage due to flooding, earthquakes, and theft, and take preventative measures to insure against these losses. To avoid gaps in coverage, you should meet with your insurance agent.

Other preventative measures

Although insurance protects against loss, it is a resource one hopes not to have to use. Like a life raft, it is better to have it and not need it, than to need it and not have it. To help prevent claims against you, take the following precautions.

- Hire licensed and insured contractors who know their trades and are safety conscious.
- Review the jobsite for unsafe conditions and make any needed corrections immediately.
- If the jobsite is in a high-crime area, consider installing a rented chain-link fence to prevent theft.
- Post "no trespassing signs" per your state's requirements for construction site signage.
- Lock all doors and windows, and do not store expensive items in the house, especially not in plain view.
- Consider lighting the jobsite during the night. This will help your neighbors spot suspicious activity so that it can be reported to the police.

And most importantly, work with professionals including licensed insurance agents who are familiar with state and federal regulations. These professionals can analyze your exposure to risk and determine whether or not your coverage (and your contractor's coverage) is sufficient.

BONDS: THE THIRD-PARTY GUARANTEE

Most people, including many contractors who claim to be "licensed, bonded, and insured," often have questions about bonding and its role in construction.

Just as a state's requirement for contractor licensing and insurance is a means to protect the public, a ***surety bond*** also offers protection because it guarantees that a person will meet his or her obligations. A third party, ***the surety***, which is informally known as a bonding company, makes this guarantee.

A surety bond is a three-party contract that exists between the following parties:
   • The obligee, who requires that an obligation be performed
   • The principal, who must perform this obligation
   • The surety, which guarantees this obligation by the principal

Surety bonds are used to guarantee the performance of an obligation. Because there are many kinds of obligations, there are many kinds of bonds that guarantee these obligations. In fact, there are thousands of bond types required by government, businesses, and individuals. In order to know what a bond guarantees, you need to read the specific language of the bond.

In construction, bonds can generally be divided into two categories:
- Contract bonds that bond the contract
- Non-contract bonds that bond non-contractual obligations

Although both categories of bonds guarantee a contractor's performance, contract bonds address a specific construction contract while non-contract bonds address the contractor's general performance.

Non-contract bonds: Contractor license bonds

Contractor license bonds fall under a broad category of license and permit bonds —bonds required by the state before an entity can do business.

Other professionals that might be regulated by permit and license bonds because their occupations can cause harm are:
- Pawnbrokers
- Auctioneers
- Motor vehicle dealers
- Real estate brokers
- Adoption agents
- Bail bond agents

Contractor license bonds, or more specifically, code observance bonds, guarantee that the applicant will abide by the laws set forth by the state, along with other applicable codes and ordinances. Consequently, the surety may be liable for a contractor's failure to comply with these requirements. Should the bonded contractor default, you may be able to make a claim against the surety for your losses caused by the default. If your claim is valid, the surety assumes responsibility for the contractor and settles the debt. The contractor must then repay this amount to the surety. But be prepared to submit significant documentation to support your claim. Contracts, payment receipts, building permits, and other documents are essential to demonstrating your case against the contractor.

A contractor license bond (or a significant cash deposit) is sometimes a requisite of contractor licensing. This bond must be kept current for the contractor to remain licensed. Consequently, the contractor pays premiums to maintain the bond, which must be active when his or her license is due for renewal. Although contractor license bonds do safeguard you from loss, only a few states require them.

Contract bonds: Bid, performance, and payment bonds

Contract bonds, like non-contract bonds, also play a limited role in *residential* construction. However, contract bonds play an enormous role in commercial and government work. And as their title suggests, they bond the contract for a specific project, rather than the contractor's general performance.

There are three main types of construction contract bonds:
- *Bid bonds* provide assurance that a contractor will enter into the proposed contract and supply any required performance and payment bonds. This reduces frivolous bidding because it requires the bidder to hold to his price or be penalized.
- *Performance bonds* provide assurance that the contractor will perform per the terms and conditions of the contract. With a performance bond in place, the owner is protected from losses resulting from a contractor's failure to perform.
- *Payment bonds* are an assurance that the contractor will pay subcontractors, laborers, and material suppliers up to the amount of the bond. This eliminates the risk of liens on an owner's private property because the surety bond acts as collateral instead of the property title.

Maintenance or warranty bonds guarantee the construction and materials for one year after completion. Although maintenance bonds can be written for longer than one year, many sureties are reluctant to enter into long-term obligations. Maintenance and warranty bonds are somewhat rare because this guarantee is typically included in a performance bond.

As with any contractual agreement, certain conditions must be met before the surety assumes responsibility for contractor damages. But if the bonded contractor defaults and you make a valid claim, the surety will ensure project completion and/or payment of legitimate claims. The surety will then look to the contractor, who has corporately and probably personally guaranteed the bond, for reimbursement.

Because insurance companies often underwrite surety bonds, these bonds are commonly mistaken as a type of insurance, such as auto or homeowner's. But there is a significant difference. In an insurance claim, the insured party is not expected to repay the insurance company. In contrast, if a claim is filed against a bond, the surety will pay a valid claim and then seek repayment from the contractor. This is referred to as "indemnification."

Prequalification protects you

Considering the protection offered by performance and payment bonds, it is surprising that they do not play a bigger role in residential construction. Unfinished projects, especially when accompanied by liens, can devastate a homeowner. The surety assumes this risk when it issues a bond. Because it recognizes the potential for loss, the surety closely evaluates bond applicants. To obtain a performance bond and a payment bond, a contractor must show a history of financial strength and solid performance. A surety evaluates several factors that can be categorized as follows:

- Capital (financial statements, work in progress)
- Capacity (résumés, contingency plans, business plans, equipment)
- Character (reputation, references, relationships)

The rigorous prequalification process assures the surety that the contractor has the capacity to complete the project per the terms of the contract and bring it to a successful completion without liens. These challenging requirements prevent many contractors from obtaining these kinds of bonds and are the reason why bonding is a valuable prequalification tool for many owners.

Contractor failure

Although the surety's screening process may be considered intense, it is necessary because of the awareness of the contractor's potential for failure. Construction is a risky business and even well-established contractors can fail. In fact, a study by Dun & Bradstreet shows a higher failure rate for older companies in comparison to newer companies.

Between the years 1990 and 1997, Dun & Bradstreet studied the failure rates of construction companies based on the age of the business:

Age of company	Failure rate
Under 5 years old	32%
6–10 years old	29%
Over 10 years old	39%

BizMiner, a leading industry analyst, found that the primary causes of contractor failure are problems related to performance, accounting, management, growth, and character. As a result, the surety evaluates these issues carefully prior to bonding a contractor. Once a contractor is approved and a bond is issued for the project at hand, the surety is proactive in preventing contractor failure when made aware of a problem. The surety may provide financial and technical assistance to the bonded contractor if trouble occurs. Should this not remedy the problem, and depending on the terms of the bond, the surety may assume responsibility and replace the contractor entirely.

Because sureties play an important role in preventing contractor failure, and they generally assume responsibility should failures occur, contract bonds are required on most government projects. Performance and payment bonds protect the government and taxpayers from the high cost of contractor default. Additionally, because public property is owned by the public and therefore generally not subject to construction liens, these bonds protect unpaid subcontractors, laborers, and material suppliers who work on these projects.

Commercial contracts may also be bonded as a means to guarantee contractor performance. Although bonding is optional, many commercial clients choose to purchase bonds because of the protection bonds provide. On some projects, the lender may require a bond.

Typical Rates for Performance/Payment* Bond Cost (2009)
- $25 per $1,000 up to the first $100,000 of the contract amount
- $15 per $1,000 up to the next $400,000 of the contract amount
- $10 per $1,000 up to the next $2,000,000 of the contract amount
- $7.50 per $1,000 up to the next $2,500,000 of the contract amount

*Performance bonds and payment bonds are often combined.

Licensed, bonded, and insured
While bonding plays a role in residential construction, its role is minor in comparison

to licensing and insurance. License bonds are only required by a few states as a requisite of contractor licensing. Performance and payment bonds are uncommon in residential construction. But should you require a performance and payment bond from your contractor, make the contractor aware of this requirement up front. This will eliminate any contractor who is not willing to obtain a bond.

Performance and payment bonds are available to all who qualify and provide assurance that the contractor will perform your project per the terms of the contract. Payment bonds serve as substitute collateral to your property and therefore protect against claims of lien. But this protection costs money. The cost of the performance and payment bonds will be added to your contractor's estimate. However, you may find the security offered by these bonds a worthwhile and affordable investment.

Because a surety must have the ability to cover the cost of contractor failure, work with a reputable surety that is financially responsible and licensed to transact surety. *The Best Key Rating Guide* (www.ambest.com) provides information about sureties' financial performance. Once you approve a surety, work directly with this company to ensure that the bond is authentic because counterfeit and fraudulent bonds do exist.

Recovery fund—another resource

States regulate contractors as a means to protect the public health, safety, and welfare but, unfortunately, even licensed contractors can cause harm. Some contractors abandon their work, leaving the homeowner with an unfinished and defective project. Consequently, some states have established a *Recovery Fund* to reimburse people who have suffered monetary losses due to the misconduct of licensed contractors. The recovery fund contains monies collected from various sources such as building permit fees and license fees.

Currently there are several states with active recovery funds; each fund is different. Arizona and Florida's recovery funds provide recourse from broad damages caused by contractors, whereas Utah and Michigan's recovery funds address loss resulting from liens. In addition, each recovery fund has different rules regarding who is covered by the fund, the type of construction that is covered, and how much can be paid out. For example, Arizona only allows claims from owners who will occupy the house as a residence. Florida excludes claims from people who buy a spec home—that is, a home that is completed before it is sold. When a claim is paid, each state's payouts vary significantly.

But applying for recovery funds is no easy matter. It is an arduous and time-consuming affair because the claimant must meet the state's stringent requirements for compensation. This may include having to prove that a contractor's mismanagement or misconduct resulted in financial harm, or that the contractor signed a false statement regarding bonding or insurance.

In addition, many supporting documents may be required to pursue a claim. These documents can include signed contracts, payment records, building permits, inspection reports, liens, and lien waivers. It must also be noted that many claims cannot be processed prior to a court judgment being issued. This requires the claimant to first pursue a claim in court—or possibly in two courts if the contractor is bankrupt—and then appeal to the recovery fund board.

Because each state's recovery fund has different requirements, it is imperative to contact your state regarding the rules for compensation and the status of the fund itself. For example, Florida currently has a shortfall of funds because of the decline of issued building permits. Consequently, although Florida is still processing claims, it is unable to pay approved claims at this time. Other state recovery funds have been found to be underfunded and may have other problems as well.

Time is of the essence

If you pursue compensation through a claim against a license bond, surety bond, or recovery fund, it is essential that you act both quickly and responsibly because there may be limited funds as well as time limitations for making a claim. When seeking reimbursement, act decisively and follow the rules set forth by the state and the surety.

8

I SPY, OH MY!

Have you ever read a captivating mystery that you just couldn't put down? Or have you been engrossed by watching TV detectives methodically solve a murder? From Sherlock Holmes to *CSI: Miami*, we are intrigued with the hidden truth—especially when the truth is revealed slowly in a well-paced drama.

The investigative process is a series of small discoveries. With thoughtful persistence, this information is accumulated until the final "ah ha" moment is reached. Many would agree that the journey is as exciting as the conclusion because the detective's methods are surprising and clever. Today, obtaining information is not nearly as difficult as it was in the past. Transparency is the trend, so much so, in fact, that people go out of their way to publish information about themselves. With this abundance of information, and the ease at which it is acquired, you won't need that cloak and magnifying glass to find clues about a contractor.

Researching your potential contractor is important because you want to hire the best person for your job. In addition to confirming that the contractor meets the state's requirements for contracting, it is also important that he or she meet certain standards of personal integrity. This is especially important when there are no state licensing and insurance regulations in place for the contractor's trade. For instance, your state's statutes may not regulate painters, carpet installers, and other tradesmen. Consequently, the burden of contractor prequalification falls on you. To determine your prospective contractor's qualification and character, public information can be reviewed. This information is readily accessible if you know where to look and what to look for.

A record of the past

There are few who would argue that "who we are today is the result of our past." When we are young, we may be foolish and carefree, but as we age, we are expected to grow wise from our life experience and knowledge. Many of our actions and accomplishments, both good and bad, are recorded in some manner. From personal blogs to government records, there is abundant recorded information that can be analyzed. These records contain information about a person's past actions, personal interests, and many other things of note. Through an investigation of a contractor, you will be able to determine if he or she has both the character and the competency to do your job. Before you begin this labor-intensive records search, know that the process, done correctly, is complicated and time-consuming. This is especially true of the review of legal information.

Records are everywhere

When you review a person's past, you are doing a background check. You, as well as an attorney or investigative service provider, can perform this investigation, and the fees for the information vary. If you do the work yourself, there may be no cost. But a thorough investigation performed by a professional can range from a modest amount to thousands of dollars.

When investigating a person's background records, it is essential to obtain as much accurate information as possible and then objectively analyze this data. Anything less and you compromise your goal, which is to accurately and fairly evaluate your contractor. Just as you do with a jigsaw puzzle, you need all the pieces and they need to be correctly assembled; anything less, the puzzle is incomplete. Additionally, some portions of your research, like some sections of a puzzle, are more easily accomplished than others.

For example, confirming a contractor's professional license is a relatively easy task because there is little to interpret. He has a license or he does not. In contrast, interpreting his legal history can be difficult if you are unfamiliar with the complicated language of the law. Without an understanding of the legal terms, abbreviations, and their meanings, a flawed interpretation may result. If you decide to proceed with an initial look at public records, make sure you understand the information and that your information is correct and inclusive. Then strive to review the information with objectivity. Your evaluation will help you determine if a contractor meets your standards for competency and character. The following information may help you get a general idea of your contractor's recorded past conduct.

Official records and public records

The government documents events in your life from the day you are born (birth certificate) until the day you die (death certificate). These documents, when required by law to be recorded, are called official records and can include documents such as liens, notices, deeds, and certificates. These various types of records are held at the federal, state, and local levels of government. Official records that are authorized by law to be available for public viewing are called public records.

In 1966, President Lyndon B. Johnson signed the Freedom of Information Act, which gave the public the right to view some of the information held by federal agencies. Each state then enacted its own freedom of information legislation, now referred to as Sunshine Laws. Because each state has unique Sunshine Laws, what is public record in one state may not be public record in another state.

The government also maintains records on itself to allow for transparency. For example, government business is recorded so that people can monitor not only potential wrongdoings of public agencies but also so that they can evaluate the efficiency of an agency and its programs. This transparency allows people to hold government accountable for its actions and helps to ensure a "government of the people, by the people, for the people."

The release of these records into the public domain is a hotly debated issue because it pits the public's right to know against a person's right to privacy. The release of records that contain information about a person's Social Security, tax, credit, medical, military, education, and criminal history is often restricted and therefore may require this person's permission before it is released to a third party. In some cases, a third party may be allowed by law to access this information with a court order. To safeguard an individual's right to privacy and thereby prevent crimes such as identity theft, each state carefully considers which records to release into the public domain and thereby make "transparent."

Florida and many other states have passed legislation that facilitates the public's access to government spending. These Transparency Acts provide for searchable online databases that document where taxpayers' money is spent. Information about federal spending is available at www.usaspending.gov.

State licensing websites

States that require contractors to be professionally licensed may also record information about contractors who have been disciplined by the state licensing board. This information is most likely held at your state's Professional Licensing Division. In addition to disciplinary actions against licensed contractors, you may be surprised to find a list of public complaints against unlicensed individuals: CONtractors. When you perform your initial search for your potential contractor's license, check to see if the website lists any disciplinary actions by the board.

States with extensive contractor licensing laws will most likely also have strict penalties for those who have violated these regulations. The penalties may range from the mandatory payment of fines to the suspension or revocation of the contractor's professional license. Punishable violations are numerous and may include improper acts such as fraud, inadequate jobsite supervision, and the abandonment of a job.

The following are some examples of construction contracting violations and their maximum punishments enforced by the Florida Department of Business and Professional Regulation in 2009.

Violation	Maximum Penalty
Obtaining a license through fraud or misrepresentation	$10,000 and revocation
Convicted or found guilty of a crime related to contracting	$10,000 and revocation
Fraudulent, deceitful, misleading representation	$10,000 and revocation
Acting under a name not on the license	$3,000 and probation or suspension
Mismanagement causing financial harm	$10,000 and revocation
Failure to supervise construction activities	$3,000 and probation or suspension
Contracting beyond scope of license	$3,000 and probation or suspension

Contracting with a delinquent license	$2,500 and probation or suspension
Abandonment	$7,500 and probation or suspension
False payment and insurance statements	$10,000 and suspension or revocation
Gross negligence resulting in danger to life and property	$10,000 and revocation

These are only some of the rules that Florida enforces to help maintain high standards for contractors. But a state can only enforce these rules if it is made aware of a contractor's improper acts. Many aggrieved homeowners do not put forth the effort and time necessary to file a claim against the contractor because of the substantial paperwork required. Some of the documents required to file a complaint might include contracts, proof of payment, building permits, permit applications, official notices, liens, and judgments. Therefore, unless there is proper documentation of the job, it may be difficult or even impossible to file an official complaint. But should the complaint be filed and the contractor found in violation of state law, not only will the contractor be subject to punishment, the injured party may obtain financial compensation from the state *if* the state maintains a recovery fund to reimburse those who have suffered financial loss from licensed contractors.

You should also consider this: By assisting the state in penalizing contractors who break state construction contracting regulations, you help the community as a whole. But this reporting system should not be used to submit false or exaggerated reports against contractors who are not in violation of state law for this very good reason: It may be a crime! For example, in Florida it is against the law to mislead a public servant and, if you are found guilty of doing so, you may be charged with a second-degree misdemeanor. Therefore, do not submit a false or embellished complaint against a contractor. To do so is unethical and possibly unlawful.

Secretary of State and the Division of Corporations

Your state's Secretary of State Office (or Department of State) is often informally known as the keeper of records because this office records and maintains many records. These records contain information about people, businesses, and the government itself.

The Division of Corporations is a division within the Secretary of State Office that accepts and maintains a business's filings. The business entities include corporations, limited liability companies, partnerships, and sole proprietors doing business under an assumed fictitious name. The documents maintained by the Division of Corporations include a company's initial registration and the subsequent annual reports, all of which contain information about the company and its officers. One purpose of these filings is to disclose to the public the legal personal names of the business's officers. Additionally, registration ensures that a business meets the state's requirements, including registering with the proper taxing authorities. Once registered, the business must continue to file an annual report or may lose its active status.

Unlike in the past, when many construction tradesmen worked for themselves without establishing a company, many now recognize the need to demonstrate a level of professionalism afforded by company ownership. For a relatively small cost and effort, a contractor can demonstrate to potential customers that he has met the state's standards for business ownership. Investigating a contractor's annual report can help you assess his company's standing with the state. This information is available at your state's Division of Corporations office and is published online in most states.

Searching the Division of Corporations' database

When using an online search engine to reach your state's Division of Corporations website, it is essential to enter relevant search words. Enter words such as "State of Florida" and "division of corporations," for example. Once the search engine returns links, review the addresses before navigating away from the search returns page. Official website addresses will most likely contain ".us," ".gov," or ".org." (You can navigate directly to your state's Division of Corporations using the website addresses provided in the appendix.)

Once you have reached the state Division of Corporations website, look for a link that allows for a search of online records. When using any database, follow all directions provided on the website to ensure accurate results. Errors in punctuation, spacing, capitalization, and spelling may affect the search returns.

Each state differs in what information is provided during this initial search and the cost for this information. Basic information usually includes the business entity's name, its status (active, inactive, etc.), the date of registration, and the registered agent for the corporation. Depending on the state, a list of corporate officers may be provided during this preliminary search. Otherwise, an additional inquiry and fee may be required for the release of this information.

Corporate Filings

When investigating a contractor's company, the status of his company's standing with the state is important. Is the company active? Is it in good standing? Or has it been repeatedly dissolved? Beware of a contractor who repeatedly dissolves his company only to open up under another company name. This may indicate a troubled past. To perform this research, you need to search records based on the contractor's personal name. Depending on the state, the database search engine may allow for this.

When you perform research based on the contractor's name, records will be returned only if he is either the registered agent or, depending on the state, a corporate officer. Therefore, if he is an employee of a company and not an officer or the registered agent, the search may be inconclusive. However, if the contractor is an officer or registered agent, you should be able to access all filings pertaining to him, including filings from other companies where he acts as the registered agent and/or the corporate officer.

It is important to understand the difference between a registered agent and a corporate officer. Although the registered agent can be a corporate officer, he or she can also be a lawyer or someone permitted to file and accept documents on the company's behalf, and may not be an owner, director, or employee of the corporation.

EXAMPLE OF A DIVISION OF CORPORATIONS' SEARCH RETURN

Florida Profit Corporation
GREAT BUILDERS, INC

Registered Agent Name		Address	
RICHARDS, CHRISTY M.		188 Main St. Anytown, FL 55582	

Filing Information

Document Number	P08I2000029944	State	FL
FEI Number	59-8987654	Status	ACTIVE
Date Filed	02/12/2005	Effective Date	02/12/2005

Principal Address
2466 Builders Rd. Anytown, FL 55583

Mailing Address
2466 Builders Rd. Anytown, FL 55583

Officer/Director Name		Address	
RICHARDS, CHRISTY M.		2466 Builders Rd. Anytown, FL 55583	

Annual Reports
1998 – 2009

Document Images

    View

Investigating a contractor's company is as important as inspecting him as an individual because both need to demonstrate a history of good behavior. Not only should the contractor and his company be qualified to perform the work, both should also demonstrate ethics and sound business practice. The Division of Corporations records can provide helpful insight into the contractor's ability to meet the state's requirements for business registration.

Online building permitting databases

Many Building Departments have an online permitting database that allows people to obtain permits and schedule inspections. Depending on the database, you may be allowed to search a contractor's permitting and inspection history based on a jobsite address, permit number, or the contractor's license number. The records may document the type of permit that was issued for each job, the inspections performed and their results, and the status of the job. The payment history for these activities may also be available.

If the database allows for these searches, you can check a contractor's inspection and payment records for re-inspection entries. Excessive re-inspections can indicate that the contractor has difficulty performing the work properly. But it must be noted that a "partial inspection," an acceptable and common event on large jobs, may be listed as a "re-inspection" in the database. Therefore you should check with the Building Department for clarification of its database terms.

Legal research on individuals and their companies

Legal research can also be used as an investigative tool because it provides information about a person's legal history as well as his company's compliance with the law—as applicable. Legal research can provide insight into a contractor's possible criminal and civil offenses such as drug abuse, theft, and bankruptcy.

The Clerk of Court Office is the government office that performs court-related duties such as the docketing and maintaining of civil and criminal records. Recorded documents (called instruments)—such as deeds, tax warrants, claims of lien, and marriage/death certificates—may also be recorded by the Clerk of Court Office or at a separate office such as the recorder's or comptroller's office. Because each government manages its records in a unique manner, the location of this information varies with each government. In the past, obtaining legal information required a visit or a phone call to the courthouse or recorder's office. Although this is still an option, today you can access much of this information online.

The recorder's office provides notice to the world regarding various items. For example, a recorded tax lien alerts the public that the federal, state, or local government has a lien on someone's property. A recorded property deed informs the public who the property owner is. In contrast, the Clerk of Court Office can be viewed as a recorder of legal proceedings documenting both pending and past court actions in the form of docket entries.

Ethics and accuracy

Issues related to the release of court records into the public domain have challenged policymakers for a long time. Many agree that the release of court records into the public domain helps protect the public. But there are obvious occasions when some records should be shielded from public view. For example, records that contain Social Security numbers and financial account data can jeopardize a person's financial security. The release of trade secrets and information regarding juveniles can also be compromising. Each state considers these issues and more when drafting policies regarding which legal records will be authorized for public viewing.

Just as the government tries to perform ethically, you also should strive for fairness as a researcher. It is important to be accurate, thorough, and objective so that you correctly assess your potential contractor. To fairly judge a person's character and qualifications, it is essential that you obtain as much information as possible. Then this information must be carefully evaluated so that your ultimate judgment is accurate. To accomplish this goal, you have to put forth time and effort. This can be especially challenging if you are unfamiliar with legal language and abbreviations.

Therefore, although legal information can help you to determine a contractor's qualifications and character, you may want to seek counsel from specialists, such as attorneys and investigative service providers, who can perform a more thorough interpretation of legal information. If you conduct preliminary research, the following methods can be used to provide general information about the person that you are investigating. Then you must determine if you are qualified to interpret this information accurately.

Court docket entries versus court records

Legal research can range from a quick look at docket entries to extensive reading of court records.

A *docket entry* is a brief note about a legal proceeding that has occurred or is scheduled to occur. For example, a docket entry could read "heard," "filed," and "issued" and be accompanied by a brief description of the event. In contrast, *court records* include pleadings, motions, depositions, and the like.

To get a general impression about a contractor's legal history, the docket entry is usually sufficient and is often available online. In contrast, court records must be requested from the Clerk of Court Office and obtained by mail or in person.

Online court docket entries

The initial challenge to finding legal information about a person is locating the specific Clerk of Court Office that maintains the information you seek. To find the proper clerk's office, you should know the following:

- The Clerk of Court Office is typically a branch of county-level government.
- Entries can be filed under a person's name and/or company name. For example, Roger Schmidt's information may be recorded under "Roger Schmidt" and/or under his company name (e.g., "Roger Schmidt Landscaping").
- Entries may be filed in the jurisdiction where the person lives, where the person owns a business, or where the action took place.

Therefore, to find the correct Clerk of Court Office you need to know:

- The contractor's name and address (including the county name)
- The contractor's business name and address (including the county name)
- The names of the counties where the contractor works

With this information, you should be able to locate the specific Clerk of Court Office where these records are held, *if they exist.*

Search tips: Reaching the correct Clerk of Court Office

With the address and county name of the contractor's home, office, and jobsites, you can use your search engine to link to the appropriate Clerk of Court Office. If the locations of the contractor's home, office, and jobsites are in various counties, different searches must be performed.

When using a search engine to locate the Clerk of Court Office, enter the search words "clerk of court" and the county name and state name. With targeted search words, your search engine should return relevant links toward the top of the list. But before you navigate, review the links for a clue where they lead. Unfortunately, county and city web addresses do not contain the helpful clue provided on most state and federal web addresses. Whereas most federal and state websites contain ".gov" and ".us" in their website addresses, county and city web addresses primarily contain ".org" or ".com." Therefore it is difficult to quickly evaluate a search engine's returns and correctly navigate directly to the government website. Instead you must select the link that looks most appropriate and then investigate the website.

Fortunately, web addresses are not the only clue as to whether you have landed on a government website. Here is another: Government websites lack private advertising! Federal government policy states that "a .gov domain may not be used to advertise for private individuals, firms, corporations or imply in any manner that government endorses or favors any specific commercial product, commodity, or service." Most state, county, and city government websites follow the intent of this policy and do not allow private advertisements on their websites.

You can also begin your search at the county's main webpage. Use your search engine or visit the National Association of Counties (NACo) website, which provides links to all the county governments in the United States. NACo is a nonprofit organization that provides services and products to county governments and the public. Its website, www.naco.org, provides information about each county's population, size, and founding date, as well as the links to the county websites. The website www.usa.gov can also help you link to local governments. This federal website contains extensive information about U.S. government, education, jobs, defense, environment, health, benefits, science, technology, and public safety.

Inside the clerk's website

Once you have reached the Clerk of Court Office, look for a link to the online records search feature. This database should allow searches by an individual's name and company name. But before you begin, be aware that the search engine will likely return only exact matches to your search criteria. To get accurate results, it is important to enter the search words as specified on the website. Spaces, punctuation, and capitalization may affect your search results. Take the time to read the search guidelines before you begin your search.

Broad search versus narrow search

Because the search engine will likely return only exact matches to the search criteria you enter, you may want to do a broad search using only the contractor's last name so that records that may exist are not excluded. Performing this broad search helps to eliminate errors that can occur if the first name is misspelled. For example, if the name "Terri" is misspelled as "Terry," records may not be returned even if they exist. If the search engine requires an entry for the first name, enter the first initial of the first name. Although this broad search method may require you to investigate multiple records to find the one you want, it will help to ensure that you find the right person and his or her records if they exist.

Two other factors that should be considered when performing a search are nicknames and married names. For example, because Bob is often a nickname for Robert, you should perform a search using both names. If you are investigating a married woman, you should perform searches using both her married name and her maiden name, if you know it. (Maiden names also can usually be found in public records.) These are important steps in the investigative process.

> *The database may allow you to specify what type of record you seek. If you leave this entry blank, a broad search will be performed and return an extensive listing of records. Performing a broad search reduces the possibility of records being omitted.*

The search returns

When you perform a search for legal information you may or may not find it. But that does not mean that it does not exist. Consider the following:

- Are you searching the correct Clerk of Court Office database?
- Did you enter the search criteria per the website's directions?
- Did you perform a broad search with the name spelled correctly?

If you used proper search techniques and information is not returned, this may be the result of several factors, such as:

- There is no legal information about this person at that office.
- The information is sealed or expunged.
- The information is not yet entered into the database.

If your search turns up no information, you must use your judgment to determine whether you have satisfactorily investigated the contractor. If the contractor has resided in the area for many years, comes well recommended by knowledgeable friends, and meets your requirements for licensing and insurance, you may decide that he is a worthy candidate. But if records are returned, it is essential to evaluate them thoroughly.

Investigate all the docket entries that pertain to the record to determine how the matter was resolved. Because interpreting legal procedures and rulings can be difficult, you may determine that an expert is required. Attorneys and private investigators can provide this service.

Also, remember to use both the contractor's personal name and his or her company name when using searchable databases. If the contractor's home and office are in different counties, you may need to access separate Clerk of Court Offices.

From government to private industry records

In addition to government records, information maintained by private entities may be useful to you during your investigation of contractor candidates. People voluntarily create records about themselves on websites such as Facebook. In other instances, records are created by another party. Note that whereas the government has well-researched and professional standards regarding its recording policy, the private industry often has less stringent standards.

User review websites

People often rely on the opinions of others to guide them when purchasing a product or service. Whether they ask a friend or use the Internet, the information obtained is often helpful because it is based on other people's experiences and insights.

Recently, user review websites have become a popular venue for the exchange of opinions and information. User review websites are for consumers, by consumers; they contain opinions about people, products, content, and other things. The opinions on these sites can be helpful, but there are times when the information is biased or false.

It is important to know that many user review websites do not restrict postings unless they contain profanity, obscenities, threats of violence, or private financial information. Also, many user review websites do not verify the information contained in the post. For instance, a contractor may be allowed to post under an assumed name and embellish his or her capabilities without providing evidence of these achievements. Likewise, a disgruntled homeowner may be allowed to submit a negative report about a contractor without providing thorough documentation supporting this claim.

Therefore, when using these user review websites, be sure to read the site's policy regarding submissions; this may give you a sense of the accuracy and relevancy of the listed opinions. While some websites publish all postings, others will publish postings only after they have been checked for accuracy. In either case, you should evaluate these websites with an objective eye to determine if the posted information is valid and pertinent to your research.

Better Business Bureau

The Better Business Bureau (BBB) is an organization that monitors companies for sound business behavior as it relates to advertising and the sale of products and services. The BBB's goal, to honestly disclose information about a company's past performance, is accomplished by compiling and evaluating data submitted by the company as well as by the public.

The BBB's *Reliability Reports* contain general information about companies and the BBB's rating of them. These ratings are based on the company's experience, time in business, licenses, government disciplinary action, and customer complaints. In 2008, more than 50,000 complaints were made against construction contractors in various trades. Complaints, which are easily filed at the BBB website, are forwarded to the company with a request that the business address the matter. The BBB will follow up with the company if no response is received within 10–15 days.

When evaluating a company, the BBB considers the seriousness and frequency of the complaints, as well as a company's efforts toward timely resolution. The BBB also provides dispute resolution services as a free or low-cost alternative to court action. Through conciliation, mediation, and arbitration services, the BBB helps to negotiate impartial, win-win solutions for all parties.

Companies can seek accreditation by the BBB as a means to demonstrate that they meet BBB standards. In order to be accredited by the BBB, a company must prove sound financial history and performance and provide proof of all state-required bonds and licenses. Once the company is accredited, it must uphold BBB standards, including making reasonable attempts to resolve all consumer complaints.

Whether a contractor is accredited or not, he or she may be listed on the BBB website. The free online *Reliability Report*, if one has been created for the contractor you are researching, is available at www.bbb.org. To perform a search, the database requires that you enter the contractor's company name, website, or phone number, in addition to the state name where the business is located. Entering a city name is optional and will limit the search. Therefore, you may want to consider entering only the state name so that a broad search is performed. This lessens the likelihood of records being excluded from the search results.

Angie's List and RipOff Report

Angie's List (www.angieslist.com) and Ripoff Report (www.ripoffreport.com) allow consumers to document their experiences with companies they have done business with. As the name suggests, the Ripoff Report contains reports about people and companies that have performed dishonorably. In contrast, Angie's List contains reports that both praise and condemn performance. Although these websites try to guarantee the accuracy and authenticity of their reports, it is up to you to verify the online claims.

Other online information sources

Sometimes simply entering a contractor's name in a search engine can provide you with relevant information. Your search may lead to his company website or to an online publication, such as a newspaper or trade journal, that contains information about him. Your search may also lead you to social networking websites such as Facebook, MySpace, Twitter, Classmates, and LinkedIn that may reveal surprising aspects of his character. From a person's hobbies to professional associations, there is a large amount of information on the Internet that can help you develop a thorough profile.

How deep to dig

With the vast amount of personal information available to the public, it is a personal decision how much time and effort should be spent investigating each contractor. You may determine that because a contractor comes highly recommended from a knowledgeable source, very little research is required. In contrast, if you know very little about the prospective contractor, you should thoroughly research his or her qualifications and character.

The Internet has become a valuable tool for this research because there is an abundant amount of information available. The challenge lies in finding accurate and relevant information. Additionally, you must have the capability to interpret this information and review it with objectivity if you are to make a fair and honest assessment. This is time-consuming to do correctly and you may decide that the cost of an attorney or investigative service provider is a worthwhile investment. Otherwise, get as much information as possible from reputable sources and strive to make fair and informed decisions based on this information.

Additional considerations

In addition to information you obtain by your own means, you may want to ask the contractor for information about himself. By requesting a list of references and professional affiliations, you will obtain insight into the contractor's qualifications and character.

References

Once your initial research of several contractor candidates has been performed and you have narrowed your selection down to a few, you should ask these contractors about their previous projects and request references. These references should include:

- Project client name and contact information
- Project location and description
- Original project budget and final cost
- Original scheduled completion date and actual completion date

Because references tend to be handpicked so as to shed a positive light on the contractor, it is important to ask the contractor to include his five most recent projects.

Once you receive these references, you should confirm their authenticity and accuracy with the clients. Ask the clients if they encountered any problems with the contractor and if they would hire the contractor again. This information will help you determine if the contractor has, for example, 30 years' experience or one year of experience 30 times.

Professional associations

When requesting references from the contractor, you may inquire about any professional organizations he or she belongs to. Just as hobbies reflect personal interests, memberships with professional associations reflect a person's work interests. Memberships with professional, trade, and business associations demonstrate that the contractor is committed to staying current with events and information that affect the construction industry. With this information, the contractor can better serve his customers and the community.

Many residential general contractors and subcontractors belong to the Home Builders Association (HBA), which updates members on changes to building codes and standards and other noteworthy topics that affect the building industry. The Associated Builders and Contractors (ABC), Associated General Contractors of America (AGC), American Subcontractors Association (ASA), and Design-Build Institute of America (DBIA) are other associations affiliated with the building industry. Additionally, a contractor may belong to a related association such as the American Institute of Architects (AIA) or American Society of Civil Engineers (ASCE).

These associations and others promote ethical standards and require their members to do business in a professional and competent manner. In addition, membership fees often cost hundreds of dollars and require the applicant to be reviewed before acceptance into the association. Because membership with a professional organization reflects an individual's commitment to the profession, it should be a consideration when hiring a contractor. A contractor's membership claim can be verified by the association by phone or online.

Conclusion

Although verifying a contractor's qualifications and character requires time and effort, it is a necessary procedure; your efforts will help ensure that your project comes in on time and on budget and is overseen by a professional with a reputation for correct and conscientious work. Although many contractors are honest people that rely on their good reputation for future work, there are some CONtractors that may try to mislead and cheat you. When this occurs, the consequences can be devastating. Even a simple repair project can lead to lawsuits, liens, and other costly issues.

Because of this potential for harm, states try to protect citizens by implementing and enforcing laws to regulate the construction industry. State-mandated licensing and insurance requirements are some of the many means to help ensure that a contractor meets certain professional standards. But the burden lies with you to confirm that the contractor meets these requirements. Simply obtaining these documents from the contractor is not enough. In order to ensure a document's authenticity, you should verify all information with state agencies, the Building Department, and other applicable entities (see the following Contractor Candidate Checklist). Additionally, you should make sure that the names on the contractor's license, insurance, and contract are identical.

A history of personal integrity and professionalism should also be established before moving forward with a contractor. With careful consideration of a contractor's credentials and character, you can establish whether or not the contractor is qualified to submit a proposal for your project.

Once you have performed your research and selected a minimum of three qualified contractor candidates, you can proceed to request proposals.

CONTRACTOR CANDIDATE CHECKLIST

☐ 1. Assemble a minimum of three contractor candidates by:
- Referrals from qualified sources
- Advertisements from legitimate sources

☐ 2. Research your state's professional licensing requirements for contractors at:
- State Professional Licensing Division
- Building Department

☐ 3. Confirm the contractor's professional licensing (if required) at:
- State Professional Licensing Division
- Building Department

☐ 4. Research your state's workers' compensation requirements at:
- State Insurance Division
- Building Department

☐ 5. Confirm the contractor's workers' compensation insurance (if required) at:
- State Workers' Compensation Division
- Building Department

☐ 6. Research your state's general liability insurance requirements at:
- State Professional Licensing Division
- Building Department

☐ 7. Confirm the contractor's general liability insurance with:
- Contractor's insurance company

☐ 8. Research the contractor's qualifications and character through:
- Public records

- State Professional Licensing Division
- State Division of Corporations
- Building Department permitting database
- Legal records

• User review websites
- Better Business Bureau's Reliability Report
- Angie's List
- Ripoff Report
- Other

• Social networking websites
- Facebook
- MySpace
- Classmates
- Twitter
- LinkedIn
- Other

• General web search inquiry

• References

• Professional association memberships

9
MAY I PROPOSE?

Now that you have performed a thorough investigation of your prospective contractors, it is time for you to switch gears from private investigator to private businessperson. To date, you have a good idea of what is to be done (the scope of work) and who will do it (the contractor short list.) Now it is time to find out what it will cost, as well as other terms of the agreement.

In order for the prospective contractors to give you their proposed costs, you must ensure that they understand what is expected of them. Their costs will not be accurate if you do not supply them with your written scope of work, building plans, and all documents pertaining to your project. Ideally this information should be exchanged on the jobsite so that the contractor can have a look around. Even a relatively small repair job, like the replacement of a water heater, may not be as straight forward as one might assume. For example, access to the water heater may be obstructed or an electrical service upgrade may be necessary. Therefore, you should ask the contractors to visit your jobsite and discuss the project with you.

Jobsite meeting
Depending on the size of your project, the jobsite visit may be brief or it may take a couple

of hours. What is important in all cases is that you are properly prepared for the meeting because many contractors do not charge for the time and money they spend preparing a proposal. Time is money so you should be thorough and get to the point.

Explaining your goal is always a good starting point. You should be ready to list the tasks you think will be needed to accomplish your goal (i.e., the scope of work). You may find that the contractor has some helpful suggestions that will improve your project or help move it along more quickly. If you accept the suggestions, make sure these changes are incorporated into all the construction documents. Remember, you want all bidders to estimate an identical scope of work or else you will not be able to compare their prices easily.

In addition to the work that must be performed, the contractors must be aware of jobsite access, storage, waste removal, and availability of water and electricity. The contractors also need to know your projected job start date, acceptable job duration, and allowable working hours, including any restrictions. For example, some communities only allow disruptive construction to take place during certain hours of the day. With a clear understanding of the work and project conditions, the contractor can create a proposal that is inclusive and accurate.

Things to consider after your jobsite meeting:
- *Did the contractor arrive on time?*
- *Does he drive a well-maintained vehicle?*
- *Was he attentive and inquisitive?*
- *Did he offer helpful suggestions?*

Fixed-price versus time and materials/cost plus proposals

Construction projects vary in complexity and, consequently, so do types of proposals and contracts. Because these are important documents, it is important that you know something about them.

A fixed-price proposal (also called a lump-sum proposal) is often used when the proposed construction work is straightforward and readily estimated. A fixed-price proposal contains a clear scope of work and a specific cost to complete this work. Unless the scope of work is changed, the price is fixed and will not change. This provides many homeowners with peace of mind.

In contrast, a cost plus proposal (or the related time and materials proposal) is sometimes submitted for projects that are less easily estimated. For example, many renovation projects contain **hidden conditions**, that is, conditions that are hidden from sight. Existing electrical wires, water pipes, and framing are examples of elements hidden behind the drywall in an existing house. Because these hidden conditions can affect a contractor's ability to accurately estimate the work, many contractors will protect themselves against possible financial loss through these types of agreements. In contrast to fixed-price proposals, which bind the contractor to a set price, cost plus proposals and time and materials proposals allow the contractor to be reimbursed for his labor, materials, and equipment (and overhead and profit if the agreement provides for this) that are incurred during the job. These amounts are typically documented on receipts and job logs and submitted with an invoice as a requisite of payment. As you can imagine, you are exposed to significantly more risk when you agree to these types of proposals because you do not know what the final cost will be.

Determining the location of a leak is sometimes tricky business because the source of the leak is sometimes far removed from where it manifests itself. Therefore a contractor may use a cost plus agreement or time and materials agreement when bidding on a job to repair your leaky roof or leaking water pipe.

The risk of overpaying

Because cost plus agreements and time and materials agreements do not contain a fixed cost, a job cost can escalate beyond what was expected. But you can protect yourself by asking the contractor to provide you with a **guaranteed maximum price (GMP)** which caps the project cost at a specified amount. You can also offer an incentive that increases your cost savings by offering a bonus if the contract price falls below the GMP. For example, if the receipts for time and materials total $20,000 and the GMP is $30,000, you could offer a 20% bonus on the savings of $10,000. Most contractors will find this $2,000 bonus an incentive to work productively.

Fixed-price proposals are common in the construction industry. If you enter into a cost plus or a time and materials agreement, it is even more important that you thoroughly research your contractor to ensure he is honest and efficient.

A unit price agreement is another type of proposal that can be used when the quantity of work or materials is difficult to estimate. Unit price agreements provide you with a unit cost for an item or activity. For example, it can be difficult to estimate the quantity of fill dirt for a building lot that has a lot of boulders that must be removed. Therefore a site work contractor may quote a unit price per cubic yard of dirt that is delivered, spread, and compacted.

EXAMPLE OF FIXED-PRICE (LUMP-SUM) PROPOSAL

PROPOSAL

AIR CONDITIONING, INC. | LICENSE: CAC 1814248
118 NW 40TH ST. ANYTOWN, FL 55583 | (555) 783-9867

DATE: *June 21, 2009*

PROPOSAL SUBMITTED TO: *Jane Homeowner*
375 Town Lane, Anytown, FL 55582
(555) 783-9867

WE HEREBY SUBMIT SPECIFICATIONS AND ESTIMATE FOR: *Remove and dispose of the existing malfunctioning air conditioner and air handler. Provide and install: New Kool-Air Model 458-1. One ton capacity 12,000 BTU and air handler.*

WE PROPOSE HEREBY TO FURNISH MATERIAL AND LABOR, COMPLETED IN ACCORDANCE WITH ABOVE SPECIFICATIONS, FOR THE SUM OF: *$4,200.00*

PAYMENT TO BE MADE AS FOLLOWS: *Deposit of $2,000. Balance upon completion.*

ALL MATERIAL IS GUARANTEED TO BE AS SPECIFIED. ALL WORK TO BE COMPLETED IN A WORKMANLIKE MANNER ACCORDING TO STANDARD PRACTICES. ANY ALTERATION OR DEVIATION FROM ABOVE SPECIFICATIONS INVOLVING ADDITIONAL COSTS WILL BE EXECUTED ONLY UPON WRITTEN ORDERS, AND WILL BECOME AN EXTRA CHARGE OVER AND ABOVE THE PROPOSAL. ALL AGREEMENTS CONTINGENT UPON STRIKES, ACCIDENTS, OR DELAYS BEYOND OUR CONTROL. OWNER TO CARRY HOMEOWNERS INSURANCE. OUR WORKERS ARE COVERED BY WORKERS' COMPENSATION INSURANCE.

WE MAY WITHDRAW THIS PROPOSAL IF NOT ACCEPTED WITHIN 30 DAYS.

PROPOSAL SUBMITTED BY: *Air Conditioning Inc. by Joe Massey - President*

ACCEPTANCE OF PROPOSAL. THE ABOVE PRICES, SPECIFICATIONS AND CONDITIONS ARE SATISFACTORY AND ARE HEREBY ACCEPTED. YOU ARE AUTHORIZED TO DO THE WORK AS SPECIFIED. PAYMENT WILL BE MADE AS OUTLINED ABOVE.

DATE OF ACCEPTANCE: *June 21, 2009*
SIGNATURE OF CUSTOMER: *Jane Homeowner*

One step at a time

When reviewing several proposals, it is important that you evaluate each proposal individually to see if it accurately reflects your scope of work and other conditions of your project. Only then should you move on and compare the proposals to each other. Although the proposals may differ in design and content, most will share key elements such as the date, customer name, description, price, and a signature area. Other standard language may address warranty, workmanship, change orders, insurance, and the proposal's expiration date. These are all important considerations even though they are often overshadowed by the price.

Low bid: Is it a bad deal?

When prospective contractors receive a well-defined scope of work and visit the jobsite to thoroughly discuss the project with you, they should have a good understanding of the job. Now they must assign a cost to the work. Contractors use unique methods to estimate their prices. There is the work itself that must be performed as well as the basic cost associated with business—costs such as overhead and profit. Although many factors can influence a contractor's final cost, you will most likely find that your chosen contractors' bids for your job will fall within 10%–15% of each other. If the range in pricing is more significant that that, you need to consider why this is so.

Unlicensed and uninsured CONtractors generally charge less because they do not have to pay the mandatory expenses of licensed and insured contractors. These expenses include not only the cost of the license and insurance, but also additional related business expenses such as filing fees, bookkeeping costs, and business taxes. Therefore, when comparing the proposals, it is important to ensure that all the contractors are insured and licensed as required by law. Although the prices of insured and licensed contractors may be higher, you receive the benefit of their meeting the state's requirements for their trade. In addition, a contractor's insurance protects you from financial loss should an accident occur. Although price is important when shopping for a service or product, always consider the possible risks and associated cost when insurance and licensing are not in place.

Another possible explanation for an unreasonably low price is the possibility that the contractor has made an error. Heed the adage, "If it looks too good to be true, it probably is," and ask the contractor to review his proposal for any missing materials and labor. Even with his assurance that the proposal is correct, beware of a CONtractor who intentionally underestimates the work in order to get the job and then tries to renegotiate a higher price while the work is under way. This CONtractor knows that people will often pay the extra amount just to avoid the delays and additional cost of hiring another contractor.

Always remember that a contractor's price is only as good as the contractor standing behind it. If your goal is to have your project completed correctly, on time, and at a fair price, generally you should **contract with a responsible contractor who submits the lowest reasonable bid**.

Payment schedule: Deposits and progress payments

Now that the price has been evaluated, it is time to look at the terms in which the sum will be disbursed. The payment schedule, also called a ***draw schedule***, establishes when sums of money are paid.

Some contractors require a deposit to cover significant "up-front" costs such as expensive equipment needed for the job. Consider an air-conditioning contractor who must purchase both the air handler and compressor to replace an existing, broken unit. If the equipment costs him $3,000 and his proposed price is $4,800, the equipment is 60% of the total job cost. Although this contractor may not ask you for a deposit to cover the equipment cost, it is not unreasonable for him to request a deposit of 30%–60%. This deposit assures him that you have a sincere desire to proceed with the project. For this reason, deposits are also referred to as "earnest" or "good faith" money.

Another issue that contractors consider in regard to deposits is their ability to repossess an item if a CONsumer refuses to pay for the contracted service or item. For example, fill dirt is difficult and costly to repossess. Worse yet, imagine repossessing a concrete slab! Additionally, many states have laws that forbid a contractor from repossessing an item, such as an air conditioner, once it is incorporated into a building. If a contractor has had a problem with a CONsumer in the past, he may be more likely to charge a deposit before commencing work.

Collecting a deposit is an acceptable business practice. However, recognizing what is fair in terms of deposit and monthly payment amounts can be challenging because you need to have some knowledge of construction costs.

In new home construction, many contractors require a 1% deposit, or a flat fee of up to $5,000, at contract signing. A large remodel job may require a deposit of 2.5% when the contract is signed. In contrast, the deposit for the replacement air-conditioning unit may range from zero to 60% of the project cost.

Additionally, the subsequent payments vary with each job. Although a small repair job may require only two payments—a deposit and final payment upon completion—expect to make several payments during a larger job. These progress payments, and the requirements for each payment, must be known before the contract is signed. This information may be detailed on the draw schedule.

Lenders know construction costs

Because loans are often used to finance construction projects, lenders thoroughly study the costs associated with construction. Lenders look at the cost of various construction activities, such as framing, roofing, etc., and compare these individual costs to the cost of the entire job. With this information, a percentage amount can be assigned to each construction activity. Subsequently, this enables the lender to disburse a loan in sums that are proportionate to the value of the work being performed.

A construction draw schedule details what work must be completed before you can apply for payment, as well as the percentage of the total loan amount to be paid at that time. It is a *schedule of values*. Each lender has a unique draw schedule that may vary in the number of payments and the requirements for these payments, as well as payment amounts.

EXAMPLE OF A LENDER'S DRAW SCHEDULE FOR NEW CONSTRUCTION

ACTIVITY	AMOUNT
SLAB = 15% (of loan amount)	
1. Permits, rough grade, foundation survey, slab pour	15%
LINTEL = 10%	
2. Single-story construction	
a. All exterior walls in place and ready for trusses	10%
3. Two-story construction	OR
a. First-floor exterior walls in place	4%
b. Second-floor joists and subfloor	3%
c. Second-floor exterior walls	3%
FRAMING = 20%	
4. Interior wall framing	3%
5. Roof dry in	3%
6. Electrical wiring rough in	3%
7. Heating and air-conditioning ducts installed	3%
8. Bathtubs set	2%
9. Windows installed	3%
10. Finish roof	3%

ACTIVITY	AMOUNT
DRYWALL = 20%	
11. Insulation installed	3%
12. Drywall hung	4%
13. Drywall finish and texture	4%
14. Tile work (tub and shower)	4%
15. Exterior siding, stucco, brick	5%
TRIM OUT = 25%	
16. Interior and exterior paint	3%
17. Interior trim and doors including garage door	5%
18. Cabinets and vanities	4%
19. Heating and air conditioning complete	3%
20. Plumbing complete	2%
21. Electrical complete	3%
22. Sidewalks and driveway	2%
23. Landscaping and sod	3%
FINAL = 10%	
24. Wallpaper/mirrors/aluminum work	2%
25. Appliances	2%
26. Floor covering	4%
27. Screening/final clean/miscellaneous	2%

Lenders will also review inspection results, the jobsite, and any noteworthy filings such as liens as a basis for payment.

Contractor-drafted draw schedules

Although construction loans are often used to finance a construction project, they are not the sole source of project funding. Banks also offer other sources of financing, such as lines of credit, that may not require the use of a draw schedule. In addition, you may not need a loan at all. If a lender's draw schedule is not used as a basis to disburse funds, you and the contractor must agree upon the payment terms. Often this information is included in the contractor's proposal and requires you to determine if the payment terms are fair.

It is generally in your best interest to ***pay several modest amounts so that neither you, nor the contractor, is owed a substantial amount of work or money.*** Although it is reasonable for a contractor to use your money to build your project, you do not want to pay him so much that he lacks incentive to finish your job promptly or abandons your job altogether.

Front-loading

Unless you are knowledgeable of construction and its cost, it may be difficult to determine how much should be paid when. Therefore, it is important to compare the payment terms of several proposals and note any substantial differences. Pay particular attention to a proposal that requires significant payment up front in comparison to the other proposals that do not.

A **front-loaded** draw schedule pays the contractor more than the value of his work at the early stages of the project. The following is an example of a front-loaded draw schedule for the construction of a $60,000 swimming pool.

% OF CONTRACT AMOUNT	COMPLETED ACTIVITY
20%	Contract
30%	Permit documents Excavation and forming Steel placement
30%	Electric (rough) Plumbing (rough) Concrete placement
20%	Form removal, backfill, and grade Electric (final) including equipment Plumbing (final) including equipment Coping and tile Interior finish Pool filled with water

In this example, the contractor will receive $12,000 for simply bidding the job and executing the contract, a nice sum considering that the permit documents may not have been prepared. Many reputable pool contractors only require a maximum of 10% at contract signing and they generally prepare the permitting documents for this fee. Notice that the front-loaded draw schedule allows the contractor to bill for $30,000—half of the contract amount—by the second draw when all that is provided is a hole with steel in it. This amount exceeds the value of the work performed at that point, which can put you at a disadvantage. If you are owed work, a contractor may have little incentive to work swiftly because he has already been paid for this work. Additionally, if he is a real scoundrel, he may take your money and run.

In contrast to a front-loaded draw schedule (as outlined above) the Association of Pool and Spa Professionals (APSP) recommends a more equitable agreement such as the following:

% OF CONTRACT AMOUNT	COMPLETED ACTIVITY
10% deposit	Contract Permit documents including site plan and engineering
30%	Excavation and forming Steel placement Electric (rough) Plumbing (rough)
25%	Concrete placement Form removal, backfill, and grade
15%	Electric (final) including equipment Plumbing (final) including equipment
15%	Coping and tile
5%	Interior finish Pool filled with water

It is important to obtain several bids from reputable contractors because front-loading often becomes evident when the proposals are compared. It must be noted that while many contractors charge a fair amount with equitable terms, a CONtractor will try to get as much money as fast as he can and may abandon your job. ***Therefore, evaluate the proposed price as well as the payment terms carefully and, when possible, seek advice from construction professionals knowledgeable about job costs.***

Be aware that your state may have laws that limit the amount of deposits. For example, California and Nevada limit pool deposits to 10% or $1,000—whichever is less.

Other considerations

Although price and payment terms are important matters, there are other significant issues that should also be addressed and set forth within the proposal. What if the swimming pool pump fails to function, or perhaps the contractor takes an exceptionally long time to finish your project? Unexpected surprises are best saved for birthday parties and Christmas, not construction projects. So consider the following issues and make sure you have a game plan in place before you move forward with a contractor.

Warranty

When you make a purchase, you expect the product or service to function properly. Although warranties are very important, proposals often address them only briefly, if at all. Both the work and equipment should be warranted so that you are protected against faulty products and service. (Warranty provisions are addressed more extensively in the following chapter about contracts.)

Permitting

The Building Department enforces the state's building codes and construction contracting laws through the permitting and inspection of construction. Building permits, and the required inspections, regulate who can do the work, how they do it, and where they do it. When a permit is obtained, trained professionals—whose role it is to ensure the public's safety—review your project. Permits ensure that your project meets state building codes and laws pertaining to construction contracting. This protects you, and the public, from harm that can occur from unlicensed CONtractors and work that is not code compliant.

Every state has unique laws that address which construction activities require permitting. Most states require permitting of construction that includes structural, electrical, and plumbing components. Some small repair projects may be exempt from this requirement.

Because permitting requirements vary widely from state to state, you should ask your Building Department if your project requires a permit. If a permit is needed, it is important that the contractor obtains the permit and thereby assumes responsibility and liability for the job. If you pull the permit, you assume the role of contractor and the ac-companying responsibilities and liabilities for the project. Beware of a CONtractor who insists that permits, when required, are unnecessary, costly, and delay the project. He is trying to avoid complying with the state's requirements for construction and contracting.

Schedule

Given that your time is valuable, you do not want to waste it. Homeowners frequently complain that their construction project takes much longer than they had imagined, or perhaps were even told. Therefore you should discuss the construction schedule with your contractor and make sure this information is included in the proposal. Completion dates for small projects, such as the replacement of an air-conditioning unit, are usually relatively easy for the contractor to predict; time frames for larger projects can be more difficult to gauge. In any case, a completion date should be included with the contractor's proposal; without a written completion date, your project may take longer than you thought.

Entering into contract

Now that you have reviewed several contractors' credentials, character, and proposals, you must decide who to hire for your project and then enter into a legally binding contract.

Contracts vary in size and complexity, often reflecting the size and complexity of the job. Frequently, a signed proposal is used to contract a small project. In contrast, a highly detailed contract is used to bind more extensive projects, such as a home remodel or new construction. What is important to note is that both documents, once signed, become legally binding. You and the contractor are bound to the conditions set out in the docu-ment—nothing more, nothing less. Therein lies the problem with a signed proposal: most proposals are not concise or complete. They lack essential detailed information about licensing, insurance, permitting, schedule, and warranties, as well as a critical element, namely, the general conditions of the project. *General conditions* address the performance of the contracted project, including information regarding default, and should be included in every agreement. If a signed proposal is used as the contract, you should include a document that contains the general conditions as described in the following chapter.

10

CONTRACTS

Legal Disclaimer/Important notice to readers: *The following overview of contracts is presented as general information only.* It is not legal advice, *that is, the application of law to an individual's specific circumstance. To be sure that you are adequately protected by a contract,* it is essential to obtain competent legal counsel *to discuss the facts of your specific situation.*

Once you have selected a contractor, a contract must be drafted that binds you and your contractor to the terms and conditions of your job. The contract should describe who is doing what, as well as where and when the work will be performed. In addition, the contract should set forth how the contracting parties will perform the project by outlining their rights and duties. These general conditions also establish what constitutes default by the parties, as well as describe what action will be taken upon default. Once the contract is signed, each party is legally bound by its terms. The finished product will be no greater or lesser than what the contract sets forth, unless the contract allows for authorized changes known as change orders.

Contracts in general

Because a contract is a legal document that may contain complex content, this content should be presented properly. A contract should be a written (preferably typed) document instead of a verbal agreement so that material evidence of it exists. The content should also be well organized. Extensive contracts are generally divided into main topics, called articles, which are further subdivided into sections that contain the provisions of the contract. The index, which serves as a table of contents, allows for quick navigation within the contract and requires that the contract's pages be numbered.

 It is a good idea to have both contracting parties initial each page so that neither party can later claim that pages were missing from the contract he or she signed.

Lengthier contracts often include a summary that generally sets forth specific information about the project such as:
- Date of the agreement
- Names and addresses of the contracting parties (and architect if applicable)
- Jobsite address
- Scope of work and exclusions
- Schedule
- Price and payment terms

Much of this information is often summarized by short-form names as a means to shorten, and promote understanding of, a contract. These short-form names are then used throughout the remainder of the contract.

Examples of short-form names could be:
- Bob Perry, a single person (hereinafter referred to as "OWNER")
- Thomas Builders (herein referred to as "CONTRACTOR")
- Construction of Perry residence at 256 New Homes Way, Finetown, FL 45772 (herein referred to as "PROJECT")
- Building Plans by Architect FineDesign. Project# 08-0317 Perry Residence. Pages A0.01–S5.01. Last edit: 5-8-08. (Herein referred to as "CONSTRUCTION DOCUMENTS")

Because the summary defines the essence of the project, it must be correct and specific. Notice that the building plans, which often undergo several revisions, include the date of the last revision and other identifying features such as the architect's name and project title. The project location should also be correctly identified by a street address, property ID number, or legal description.

I read you loud and clear

Even though most projects are completed without incident and the contract is never called into question, it is vital that you understand and agree with the contract terms in case a dispute occurs. To promote understanding of the contract, the written language should be clear and set forth in short sentences. Contracts often contain specialized words. *Legalese*, or legal writing, contains both archaic and foreign words that may be unfamiliar or difficult to understand. Because legal writing is complex and technical, there is a trend toward making legal documents more reader friendly. This trend is known as the "Plain English Movement." But even the use of plain English may not make clear some complex provisions such as "indemnity clauses" and "waivers of subrogation." Subsequently, many complex contracts are signed before they are thoroughly understood. This can have grievous consequences because there is often no legal recourse if you fail to read or comprehend a contract. If you are at least 18 years old, can read, and are of sound mind, you are generally bound by the contract you signed.

There are some occasions where law may allow you to cancel a contract after you have agreed to it. For example, you may have a "three-day right to cancel" if you purchased goods or services during the course of a home solicitation sale. Likewise, you may be entitled to a "three-day cooling-off period" if you contracted for services performed on a continuing basis. Information about consumer protection laws can be found in your state statutes and at consumer agencies.

Complex language is not the only thing that can hinder the understanding of a contract. Contracts that contain extensive provisions often go unread because contract review can be tedious and time consuming. Contracts that address almost every incident that can occur during construction often seem intimidating and confrontational. In contrast, contracts with fewer provisions may fall back on *implied terms* to prevail where the contract is silent and absent of specific provisions. For example, in Florida the following terms are implied by law in a construction contract:

- The contractor has the duty to exercise skill and care as needed (i.e., good workmanship).
- The contractor will perform the work in a reasonable time frame.
- The contractor will be paid upon completion of the work.
- Neither party will knowingly or unreasonably hinder the other party's performance.

- Each party has agreed to perform in accordance with local custom.
- Each party agrees to a covenant of good faith, fair dealing, and reasonableness.

The *less is more* contract is often used on small, routine jobs that do not involve a substantial amount of time or money. Larger and more costly jobs often rely on more sophisticated and detailed contracts.

Implied contracts *are formed when one party accepts something of value from another party knowing that this party expects compensation. For example, if you visit a doctor and refuse to pay for the services provided, you may be breaching an implied contract because it is understood that the doctor is to be compensated for her service. Likewise, if you allow a painter to paint your house knowing that you have no agreement with him, you may be responsible for paying him. In contrast, an* **express** **contract** *specifically states the contractual agreement instead of implying it.*

Contract provisions

It is important to recognize that because every construction project is unique in some way, every contract is unique as well. Contracts vary in content, complexity, and design. While a simple repair contract may be a one- or two-page signed proposal, the contract for the construction of a new house may be eight to fifteen pages in length and contain an assortment of provisions.

Because of the number of provisions that may be included in a contract, it is impossible to address every one that you may encounter. Therefore, the following information is offered as a broad overview of provisions that *may* be contained in a construction contract. This content is for informational purposes only and is not a substitute for legal advice.

Many people use contracts drafted by the American Institute of Architects (AIA). These detailed contracts, created by construction professionals and lawyers, are updated regularly. Additionally, your contractor may provide you with his "tried-and-true" contract. With an unsigned contract in hand, a knowledgeable construction attorney can adapt it to your particular needs, the project requirements, and applicable laws, if necessary.

Possible work provisions

The work provisions within a contract define the completed project as well as activities required to complete the project. This section of the contract may be titled "Scope of Work" and it may reference the building plans and any construction documents tied to your project. If further clarification of work is necessary, it should be addressed in this part of the contract. For example, the building plans may not specifically address the following items:

- Labor
- Materials
- Equipment
- Permits and notices
- Jobsite supervision
- Onsite storage
- Temporary electric, water, lighting, and toilet
- Clean up of work area and dumpster
- Payment of all required taxes

As a result, the contract must specify whether these items are included in the contract. Excluded items that might be mistakenly thought of as included in the contractor's scope of work should also be clarified in the contract. Excluded items may include:

- Loan
- Building plans
- Real property (i.e., land or real estate—if the contractor is only building the house and not providing the lot)
- Surveys
- Engineering
- Soil testing
- Utility connections
- Closing costs

In addition to identifying what work will be performed, a contract may define how the work will be performed by including language such as: "All work will be performed in an expeditious and workmanlike manner according to standard trade practices and applicable building code requirements." A contract may also contain language that ensures that reasonable safety precautions are taken when performing the work and that the contractor abides by applicable safety laws.

Remember that the contract should clearly describe any documents that are not physically attached to it. For example, because building plans are generally not physically attached to a contract, the contract's reference to the building plans should include a title, date of last revision, and architect's name.

Possible payment provisions

A contract's payment provisions state the contract sum, and define how, when, and under what conditions this sum will be disbursed during the project.

Because money is generally exchanged for a contractor's services, a contract may require you to provide the contractor with evidence of your ability to pay for the project. Once it is established that money (or some other consideration) will be exchanged for the work performed, most contracts describe how the contractor should request payment. Supporting documents are often a requisite of payment and may include a "schedule of values" that details the work done to date and its value. Additionally, the contractor may be required to provide evidence that work was done per building code and per the terms of the contract. Therefore lien waivers and proof of approved inspections may be a prerequisite of payment. (Liens and lien waivers are discussed in Chapter 13.)

Once the payment request process is clarified, many contracts go on to specify who can authorize payment and how quickly the payment will be made. Because contractors need money to keep the project going, a contract may require the prompt payment of contractor invoices.

Prompt payment may be required by law as evidenced by the Florida Construction Contract Prompt Payment Law. Check your state's law to verify your payment obligations to your contractor (and his payment obligations to others as well).

Unfortunately, construction projects do not always go as planned and there may be disagreements between the contracting parties. These possibilities are often addressed in a contract. For example, if you do not pay the contractor for work performed per the contract terms, the contractor may have the right to stop work. But many would agree that there are occasions when payment should be withheld from the contractor; these situations are often described in the contract. Payment is sometimes withheld from the contractor when:

- There is an abundance of defective work.
- The contractor fails to pay subcontractors and material suppliers.

- There is evidence that the contract schedule and price will not be met.
- There is a substantial breach of contract.

The final payment, and the work required to obtain this payment, is an important element of a contract. This is a hotly debated topic because it is difficult to determine exactly when a project is complete and the final payment due. Project completion is a complicated matter because there is no such thing as a perfect home. Try as he might, a contractor does not always meet your expectations. Sometimes the deficiencies are significant, such as a broken swimming pool pump. Other times the defects are minor, such as a scratched wall or a door handle that does not operate properly. Because of the potential for dispute, many states have enacted laws that describe what constitutes **substantial completion**.

In Florida, substantial completion is reached when the project can be used for its intended purpose. For instance, a screen room that is missing a door latch could be considered substantially complete, whereas if it is missing the screens, it is not substantially complete. In new home construction, substantial completion is often reached when the Building Department issues a Certificate of Occupancy (CO). A Certificate of Occupancy is issued once the work is completed in accordance with the building plans and per building codes. Because not all construction projects result in the issuance of a Certificate of Occupancy (for example, a kitchen remodel, because the Certificate of Occupancy was issued when the house was initially built), other events can be used to gauge the substantial completion of a project. A Certificate of Completion (CC) or an approved final inspection of the work may also constitute substantial completion.

Each contract has unique provisions for final payment. A contract may require payment of the entire amount upon substantial completion. If minor defects need to be remedied, the contractor should acknowledge the **punch list** (a list of these deficiencies) and agree to repair them quickly. Because work is owed you, you may want to have the contractor sign a written document stating this agreement. An alternative sequence of events may be that the deficiencies are corrected and then final payment is made. In this case, there may be a provision that limits you to one punch list so that you do not continually add to the list of deficiencies and thereby prolong the project. The contract may also prohibit you from moving into the house until after this work is completed and the contractor is paid.

Other conditions for final payment may also include:
- Written acceptance by the architect
- Owner's receipt of all warranties and manuals
- Final lien release and final payment affidavit from the general
  contractor as well as final lien releases from all lienors

Because the final payment is an important element of the contract, its terms should be reviewed closely.

Changes in contract price

During the course of construction, changes to the original scope of work and contract price may occur. Change may be necessary for a number of reasons. Perhaps you simply desire a change while construction is under way. Other times the change is unavoidable, such as when an unknown or hidden condition becomes evident, building materials become unavailable, or errors are discovered in the building plans.

Because changes often occur, it is important to define the means that allow for these changes. Generally, contracts allow for change through a written change order that must be signed by you and your contractor. The assignment of cost for the change order may also be addressed in the contract. You may be responsible for costs resulting from unknown conditions such as hidden boulders in your soil. But if the change order is the result of contractor (or architect) error, the contract may assign the cost of this change order to the party at fault. Because change orders can be costly, their provisions should be thoroughly reviewed before the contract is signed.

Possible schedule provisions

Schedule provisions address the project's start date and duration. The start date can be stated as a specific date or as a number of calendar days after an event such as loan closing or issuance of a building permit. The completion date, on the other hand, is more difficult to determine on large projects because a contractor often relies on factors beyond his control. These factors can include weather, unknown conditions, and material shortages. The schedule can also be affected by the performance of other parties such as subcontractors, who may become injured or ill. Therefore, although residential construction contracts often contain a proposed completion date, the contract may also include language that only obligates the contractor to make a "good faith effort" toward achieving this goal.

But because good faith may not equate to timely performance, many contracts include provisions that require prompt action by the contractor when he or she encounters situations that can lead to delay. If unknown conditions become evident or errors in the building plans are discovered, the contractor must quickly bring these matters to light. You must also act promptly when called upon to make decisions. When both parties are obligated to act in a timely manner, the project is likely to move forward at a reasonable pace.

Possible insurance provisions

Insurance is addressed in most contracts because of its importance. Many contracts outline the types of insurance required by the parties as well as the amount of required coverage. Often the contract requires the contractor and any hired subcontractors to have general liability and workers' compensation insurance. You may be required to purchase a builders' risk policy. Because the insurance clause is such an important and often complex element of the contract, it is strongly recommended that you ask an insurance agent to review these provisions.

Possible warranty provisions

Warranty provisions address a contractor's promise to repair or replace any faulty work, material, or equipment for a specific period of time. In construction, warranties often fall into two categories: manufacturer's warranties and builder's warranties.

Manufacturer's warranties cover equipment and appliances in the home and are warranted by the manufacturer. New refrigerators, washing machines, and dishwashers are examples of appliances generally covered by a manufacturer's warranty. Roofing shingles and vinyl siding are examples of building materials generally covered by a manufacturer's warranty. In contrast, the contractor generally warrants workmanship in the builder's warranty. The builder's warranty may also cover general building materials and the building systems such as electric, plumbing, and heating, ventilating, and air conditioning (HVAC). Although most builders offer a basic one-year warranty, many builders offer a more extensive warranty policy provided through a third-party national company such as Bonded Builders Warranty Group, 2-10 Warranty, or Professional Warranty Service Corporation (PWC). These policies generally cover workmanship and materials for one year; limited items of the electrical, plumbing, and HVAC systems for two years; and structural elements, such as trusses and the load-bearing portions of the foundation, for up to ten years. These extensive policies may also be offered by the construction company itself if it is large enough to have the financial resources to be self-insured. Because most warranties only guarantee the reliability of the item under normal use, they usually do not cover claims that result from Acts of God or abuse. If the warranted item has been altered or repaired by others, this may also void the warranty. Be sure you fully understand what type of warranty the builder will provide before you sign the contract.

In addition to the written *express warranties* listed above, you may be protected by *implied warranties* that are assurances granted by common law. For example, when you buy a product or service, it is supposed to be fit for its intended purpose For example, a water heater should heat your water when it is properly installed. These consumer protection laws are generally contained in a state's Uniform Commercial Code (UCC). But you may also be protected by state laws known as the Statute of Repose. These statutes of limitation establish a time period in which a contractor can be held liable for improvements made to your property.

Because warranties provide valuable protection, it is important to understand what is, and is not, warranted as well as the terms of the repair or replacement. It is also important that the company providing the warranty is financially sound and responsible so that should you submit a legitimate claim, the warranty company will fulfill its obligation to you.

Possible indemnity provisions

Hold Harmless or Indemnity Agreements are some of the most powerful provisions in a contract because they address liability. In fact, the very words "hold harmless" should alert you to the need to thoroughly read and understand this provision.

An Indemnity or Hold Harmless Agreement is used by one party to pass liability (for damages) to another party. For example, a skydiving company may ask a customer to sign an Indemnity Agreement so that the company may be held harmless if the customer is injured and attempts to be compensated for this injury. Because liability and financial loss can occur during a construction project, some construction contracts contain Indemnity and Hold Harmless provisions, and they often protect the contractor.

Indemnity and Hold Harmless provisions can have grievous consequences if they are broad and one-sided. Consider the following indemnity clause that attempts to remove all liability regardless of fault:

> *"The Owner shall indemnify and hold harmless the Contractor from all damages and losses resulting from the work of the Contractor, Subcontractors, or anybody directly or indirectly employed by the Contractor."*

Imagine if you hired a contractor who, in turn, hired his unlicensed and untrained brother to install your water heater. If the water heater is improperly installed and causes severe water damage to your house, the contractor might not be liable for damages if your contract included an indemnity clause.

Indemnity provisions can come in many shapes and sizes. Some favor the contractor, some favor the owner, and some provisions try to find the middle road by assigning liability based on fault. Some contracts do not address indemnity at all. However, if indemnity provisions do exist in your contract, read them carefully.

Default, termination, and damages

Because contracts often contain numerous provisions that must be met by the contracting parties, it is not surprising when a party fails to fully comply with the contract terms. While most shortcomings are quickly remedied, others are not and can lead to the termination of a contract. Because default can have serious consequences, many contracts contain specific language that addresses it.

Sometimes when a party is in the wrong, he or she may not be aware that provisions of the contract are not being met. Therefore, it is only fair to inform the offending party in a timely manner. A written "Notice of Default" does just that and it must often be delivered per the terms of the contract, e.g., via certified mail within 10 days. The contract may also grant the contractor the right to remedy the defect before court action can be pursued. This is known as the "Right to Cure." But unfortunately, not all stories have a happy ending.

Some breaches of contract are so significant that they lead to the termination of the contract. For example, some contracts allow the contractor to terminate the agreement if he is not paid for work performed per the contract's terms. The contract may also set forth the conditions that allow you to terminate the contract. Contractor behavior that could be cause for termination:

- Consistent failure to supply satisfactory work and material
- Persistent disregard for laws, codes, and rules
- Failure to pay subcontractors and suppliers

The damages that result from the termination of a contract may also be addressed in the contract. If you default on the contract and damages are owed the contractor, the contract may award the contractor money owed to date plus a reasonable amount for lost profit, overhead, and hardship. On the other hand, if the contractor defaults on the contract, you may be entitled to money from the contractor per the terms outlined in the contract.

Dispute resolution

Because the reason for default is not always clear, many contracts set forth procedures used to help resolve this matter. Good-faith negotiations are often a required first step toward dispute resolution. If negotiations fail to resolve the dispute, private mediation may provide results. Mediation proceedings are held by a neutral third party who listens to each side and tries to fashion a remedy that is fair to both. The cost of mediation is generally shared by both parties and performed within 30 days of failed good-faith negotiations. Although the decision of the mediator may be nonbinding, it is generally in the interest of the parties to accept the decision so as to avoid future legal costs. Mediation is popular because it is less costly and time consuming than going to court. Additionally, there are fewer formalities and rules, and that makes the process easier. Because of the backlog of civil cases that may take up to a year or longer to be processed, and because legal action can be costly, many contracts contain provisions that mandate mediation prior to going to trial.

Arbitration is ordinarily seen in larger jobs and is comparable to a judgment in a court of law. Arbitrators are generally experienced contractors, engineers, attorneys, and other professionals who render decisions based on their professional experience. Generally, arbitration must be conducted according to the rules outlined by the American Arbitration Association.

Litigation takes place in the civil court where the facts in dispute are resolved by either a judge or a jury. A bench trial by a judge is generally less complicated than a juried trial by peers, and is therefore often preferred. Litigation can be costly when the matter involves defective construction because expert witnesses, such as architects and engineers, are often needed to testify. In this case, litigation costs can, and often do, exceed the damage amounts being claimed in the case. In addition, even when the prevailing party is awarded a judgment, the judgment may never be collected. Therefore, it is often recommended that negotiations, mediation, and other means of dispute resolution take place before resorting to litigation.

The contracting parties

As you can see, contracts can be complicated and they take time to create and to review. This is a wasted effort if the contracting parties do not have the authority to enter into contract. If you are contracting with a business entity, you need to make sure that the person signing the contract has the authority to bind the company. If not, you may be contracting with a tradesman, instead of a company.

Corporations, like individuals, have the capacity to enter into a contract as long as the person signing the contract has the authority to do so. Generally, a corporation's bylaws list the people that have the authority to legally bind the corporation and under what circumstances they may execute a contract. Therefore, a contractor should clarify the relationship between himself and the company by including the company name, his name, and his title when signing. For example:

Great Builders, Inc.,
by Christy Richards, President

The all-important contract

Contracts are essential because they set forth the terms and conditions of the project. Once executed, most contracts are filed and not referred to again because most projects are completed without significant problems. But occasionally problems do arise and the need for a concise and comprehensive contract becomes clear. If the contract is ambiguous and incomplete, the parties do not have the information needed to resolve the dispute. The resulting discussions rely on "he said, she said" and are time consuming and unproductive. Subsequently, these contracts often end up in court for interpretation. On the other hand, if the contract thoroughly describes the contracting parties' rights and duties, the dispute is likely to be quickly resolved by the contracting parties themselves.

As important as a concise and inclusive contract is the recognition that a contract is generally legally binding once signed. Surprisingly, people generally ignore provisions that they do not understand. Some people do not even bother to read the contract at all! *Although contract review is tedious and takes time, the agreement must be thoroughly understood.* If unclear language exists, ask for a revised contract that contains clear and ordinary (nonlegal) words. If you do not agree with provisions in the contract, do not sign it. Instead, make needed corrections in red ink and resubmit the contract for approval. You may find that a knowledgeable construction attorney can help you with this task. The expression "an ounce of prevention is worth a pound of cure" applies here because sometimes the homeowner who does not pay a modest amount for a contract review pays more for the project as a consequence of agreeing to a bad deal. A knowledgeable construction attorney can advise you of potential liabilities and help negotiate and draft a fair contract.

11
PERMIT ME TO EXPLAIN

Up to this point, you have been dealing with individuals in the private sector that may include architects, contractors, and attorneys. Now it is time for the local government to step in to ensure that both the work and workers meet state standards. Even you, if acting as your own contractor, must meet certain standards set forth by the state.

The Building Department is the state's first line of defense against unlicensed and non–code compliant construction. Through the permitting and inspection of construction work, the state regulates who does the work, how they do it, and where they do it. This requires the participation of a number of trained professionals, such as plan reviewers, urban planners, and building inspectors, who occupy positions within the municipal government. These professionals and others will review your project specifically but they will also consider how your project impacts the entire community. Your project is part of a much bigger picture and it must fit within this comprehensive design that addresses the community's safety, functionality, and quality of life. To accomplish this goal, several specialists must review your project.

In addition to the Building Department, which reviews the building plans for structural integrity and overall code compliancy, the following departments are often involved with the permitting of a new home:

- Zoning Department (and/or Planning Department), which reviews the type of building (residential, commercial, industrial, mixed use, etc.) and its location on the lot as well as within the community. This is broadly defined as "land use."
- Public Works Department (and/or Engineering Department), which reviews the project's road access and drainage. If the project is located in an area prone to flooding, the elevation of the building's floor (and septic tank if applicable) may need to be higher than historical flood levels or meet other conditions. In addition, the Public Works Department may oversee projects that impact environmentally sensitive land and waterways.
- Health Department, which ensures that any wells and septic systems meet state requirements.

Other government entities, such as the Fire Department and environmental agencies, may also be involved in the permitting process.

Please note that department names and functions differ at various municipal governments because each local government has a unique structure and each department performs unique duties. In a small town, the Building Department may perform all of the duties listed above. In contrast, a larger city will have numerous offices that participate in the permitting process.

Here's looking at you, Kid

In order for officials to perform their duties, they require a variety of documents that describe your project. These documents create the permitting package that is collected by the permit technician at the Building Department who then distributes it to the various departments. Depending on the nature of your project, this tech may require some or all of the following documents:

- Application
- Notice of Commencement
- Building plans
- Site plan (plot plan)
- Proof of ownership
- Engineered truss plans
- Energy calculations
- Utility affidavit
- Address notification form
- Subcontractor list
- Owner/builder affidavit
- Approved flood plain permit
- Approved water and septic permit

Although the number of documents may seem excessive, their purpose is to ensure that your project meets zoning, building, fire, and health codes.

The specific documents required for permitting depend on the nature of your project and the requirements of your Building Department. If your house is simply being re-roofed, the Building Department may not require anything more than a permit application and a Notice of Commencement. Other minor repairs or improvements may require no permit at all. Larger and more complex projects typically require a significant amount of documentation. Some of these documents, such as the building plans and site plan, may need to be stamped by a state-licensed architect, engineer, or surveyor. In addition, the Building Department may require preapproval from other departments before it accepts your permitting package. For example, the Building Department may require the approval from the Health Department for the well and septic portion of a project before it will review the building plans. This allows the Building Department to postpone the labor-intensive plans review until other subordinate requirements are first met.

Because each project has special permitting requirements, *it is important to visit the Building Department early in the process* to determine what documents you need. In fact, it is wise to consult with officials at the Building Department before you make expensive purchases such as building plans or costly materials. Consider a situation where you would not be allowed to build a structure because your property is designated as environmentally sensitive land that prohibits the construction of a building. Although this is rare, you certainly do not want to spend thousands of dollars on things that cannot be used. The Building Department can also advise you about the types of utilities available to you and where they are located in relationship to your property. Because Building Department officials know the issues that can affect your project, you should meet with them well in advance of the permitting process. To ensure that this meeting is productive, you should provide them with a clear description of your project and any pertinent information such as rough drawings, photos, and property location.

Permitting documents and their objective

The documents in the permitting package help local government establish whether the project meets state and local standards. While some documents are elementary, others are quite sophisticated.

The building permit application

The purpose of the permit application is to consolidate some basic information about the project, its location, and the participants. The application contains the names and contact information about the homeowner, contractor, architect, engineer, and lender. The property itself must also be properly identified and the project described in broad terms. Some applications require you to list the number of new light fixtures, outlets, sinks, toilets, etc., so that the permit fee can be calculated.

Notice of Commencement: A notice before you begin

Before a construction project commences, it is important to let the public know about it by recording a notice that becomes public record. The Notice of Commencement (NOC) is a legal document that announces the commencement of work that will improve a specific property. Once the NOC is recorded at the municipal Recording Office, it becomes public record, thereby enabling any person to obtain information about the project's location as well as the homeowner, the contractor, etc. Most importantly, the NOC provides a lienor—any person with lien rights—with the information needed to properly execute a claim of lien. (Liens are discussed in depth in Chapter 13.)

Not every construction project requires an NOC. For example, an NOC may not be required if the cost for the work is below a certain amount, say $2,500. If an NOC is required, the Building Department may require a stamped copy from the Recording Office. In addition, state law may require you to post a copy of the NOC in a visible loca-

EXAMPLE OF A BUILDING PERMIT APPLICATION

APPLICATION FOR <u>RESIDENTIAL</u> PERMIT

MY COUNTY BUILDING OFFICE

12 BUSINESS SQUARE, SUITE 260, ANYTOWN, FL 55582 | PHONE NO: (555) 794-3050 FAX NO: (555) 794-3065

PROJECT # 09-1768

1 CONSTRUCTION STREET ADDRESS: *2526 Tyson Road Anytown, FL 55584*
PARCEL NUMBER OR LEGAL DESCRIPTION: *Map of Haulover S ½ Lot 15 less W. 50 Ft. PB 1 Pg 77ORB 587 Pg 289*

2 OWNER: *Christina Masters*
PHONE: *(555) 891–1433*   FAX: *(555) 891–1423*
ADDRESS: *2526 Tyson Road, Anytown, FL 55584*
FEE SIMPLE TITLE HOLDER'S NAME (IF OTHER THAN OWNER) *N/A*

3 CONTRACTOR: *IMA Contractor Inc*   LICENSE #: *CGC 087943*
PHONE: *(555) 973–0947*   FAX: *(555) 892–7985*
ADDRESS: *3546 Magnolia Way, Anytown, FL 55582* EMAIL: *IMA@IMA.com*
CONTACT NAME/EXT. *Paul Richards ext. 49*

4 ARCHITECT/DESIGNER: *D-sin Company*   LICENSE #: *AR 0487564*
PHONE: *(555) 894–7865*   FAX: *(555) 894–7866*
ADDRESS: *7876 Straight Ln, Anytown, FL 55583*   EMAIL: *info@d_sin.com*

5 ENGINEER: *Tip Top Engineers*   LICENSE #: *PE 897654*
PHONE: *(555) 785–5643*   FAX: *(555) 894–0937*
ADDRESS: *4857 Calculus Ln, Anytown, FL 55584*   EMAIL: *info@tiptopeng.com*

6 MORTGAGE LENDER: *Loaded Lenders*
ADDRESS: *7846 Bigbucks Ln, Anytown, FL 55582*
PHONE: *(555) 789–6754*   FAX: *(555) 789–6755*

7 DESCRIBE THE NATURE OF PROPOSED IMPROVEMENTS:
NEW HOME CONSTRUCTION ☐   ADDITION ☒   REMODEL ☐   SHED/STORAGE ☐
CARPORT/GARAGE ☐   OTHER (DESCRIBE) _____

8 SQUARE FOOTAGE: LIVING (AIR CONDITIONED SPACE) *1, 259 s.f.* UN-AIR CONDITIONED SPACE *N/A*

9 ESTIMATED CONSTRUCTION VALUATION (INCLUDE LABOR AND MATERIALS) *$49,200*

10 IF YOU ARE CHANGING THE USE OF AN EXISTING BUILDING, PLEASE FILL OUT THE FOLLOWING:
EXISTING USE: _____   PROPOSED USE: _____

********* **NOTICE** **********

APPLICATION IS HEREBY MADE TO OBTAIN A PERMIT TO DO THE WORK AND INSTALLATIONS AS INDICATED. I CERTIFY THAT NO WORK OR INSTALLATION HAS COMMENCED PRIOR TO THE ISSUANCE OF A PERMIT AND THAT ALL WORK WILL BE PERFORMED TO MEET ALL PROVISIONS OF LAWS AND ORDINANCES REGULATING CONSTRUCTION IN THIS JURISDICTION. THE GRANTING OF A PERMIT DOES NOT PRESUME TO GIVE AUTHORITY TO VIOLATE THE PROVISIONS OF ANY OTHER APPLICABLE STATE OR LOCAL CODES AND/OR ORDINANCES. ADDITIONAL RESTRICTIONS APPLICABLE TO THIS PROPERTY MAY BE FOUND IN THE PUBLIC RECORDS OF THIS COUNTY. ADDITIONAL PERMITS MAY BE REQUIRED FROM OTHER GOVERNMENTAL ENTITIES SUCH AS WATER MANAGEMENT DISTRICTS, STATE AGENCIES, OR FEDERAL AGENCIES. I CERTIFY THAT THE INFORMATION CONTAINED IN THIS PERMIT APPLICATION IS ACCURATE AND TRUE.

Paul Richards — President IMA Contractor Inc.10-24-09   *Paul Richards*   10-24-09
TYPE/PRINT NAME OF CONTRACTOR/OWNER- BUILDER (DATE)   SIGNATURE OF CONTRACTOR/OWNER- BUILDER (DATE)

STATE OF *FL*   COUNTY OF *Orange*

THE FOREGOING INSTRUMENT WAS ACKNOWLEDGED BEFORE ME THIS *24th* DAY OF *October 2009* BY *Paul Richards*

WHO ☐ IS PERSONALLY KNOWN TO ME OR ☒ HAS PRODUCED *DL R8985746* AS IDENTIFICATION,
AND ☐ DID TAKE AN OATH ☒ DID NOT TAKE AN OATH.   *Nancy Notary*

NANCY NOTARY
COMMISSION # DO 5555555
EXPIRES: 02/17/2010

EXAMPLE OF A NOTICE OF COMMENCEMENT

Instrument prepared by: Constance Miller. Loaded Lenders

NOTICE OF COMMENCEMENT

PERMIT #: _____   TAX PARCEL #: *R153787-57869374895717898*

STATE OF *Florida*   COUNTY OF *Orange*

THE UNDERSIGNED HEREBY GIVES NOTICE THAT IMPROVEMENT WILL BE MADE TO CERTAIN REAL PROPERTY, AND IN ACCORDANCE WITH CHAPTER 713, FLORIDA STATUTES, THE FOLLOWING INFORMATION IS PROVIDED IN THIS NOTICE OF COMMENCEMENT.

1   LEGAL DESCRIPTION OF PROPERTY (AND STREET ADDRESS IF AVAILABLE):
    Map of Haulover S ½ Lot 15 less W. 50 Ft. PB 1 Pg 077 ORB 587 Pg 289
    2526 Tyson Road Anytown, FL 55584

2   GENERAL DESCRIPTION OF IMPROVEMENT(S): *Addition to existing home*

3   OWNER'S NAME: *Christina Masters*
    ADDRESS: *2526 Tyson Road Anytown, FL 55584*
    Phone: (555) 891-1433 Fax: (555) 891-1423
        a. INTEREST IN PROPERTY: *Owner*
        b. NAME AND ADDRESS OF FEE SIMPLE TITLEHOLDER (IF OTHER THAN OWNER)

4   CONTRACTOR: NAME: *IMA Contractor Inc.*
                         ADDRESS: *3546 Magnolia Way Anytown, FL 55582*
                         PHONE: *(555) 973-0947*   FAX: *(555) 892-7985*

5   SURETY: NAME AND ADDRESS: *N/A*
                         PHONE: FAX:

6   LENDER: NAME AND ADDRESS: *Loaded Lenders 7846 Bigbucks Lane, Anytown, FL 55582*
                         PHONE: *(555) 789-6754*   FAX: *(555) 789-6755*

7   PERSONS WITHIN THE STATE OF FLORIDA DESIGNATED BY OWNER UPON WHOM NOTICES OR OTHER DOCUMENTS MAY BE SERVED AS PROVIDED BY SECTION 713.13(1)(A)7, FLORIDA STATUES:
        (NAME, ADDRESS, PHONE NUMBER, AND FAX NUMBER).

8   IN ADDITION TO HIMSELF, OWNER DESIGNATES THE FOLLOWING PERSON(S) TO RECEIVE A COPY OF THE LIENOR'S NOTICE AS PROVIDED IN SECTION 713.13(1)(B), FLORIDA STATUES:
        (NAME, ADDRESS, PHONE NUMBER, AND FAX NUMBER).

9   EXPIRATION DATE OF NOTICE OF COMMENCEMENT (THE EXPIRATION DATE IS ONE (1) YEAR FROM THE DATE OF RECORDING UNLESS A DIFFERENT DATE IS SPECIFIED).

WARNING TO OWNER: ANY PAYMENTS MADE BY THE OWNER AFTER THE EXPIRATION OF THE NOTICE OF COMMENCEMENT ARE CONSIDERED IMPROPER PAYMENTS UNDER CHAPTER 713, PART I, SECTION 713.13, FLORIDA STATUTES, AND CAN RESULT IN YOUR PAYING TWICE FOR IMPROVEMENTS TO YOUR PROPERTY. A NOTICE OF COMMENCEMENT MUST BE RECORDED AND POSTED ON THE JOB SITE BEFORE THE FIRST INSPECTION. IF YOU INTEND TO OBTAIN FINANCING, CONSULT WITH YOUR LENDER OR AN ATTORNEY BEFORE COMMENCING WORK OR RECORDING YOUR NOTICE OF COMMENCEMENT.

SIGNATURE OF OWNER *Christina Masters*   PRINT OWNER'S NAME: *Christina Masters*
    Note: per section 713.13(1)g, Florida Statutes "Owner must sign... and no one else may be permitted to sign in his or her stead."
STATE OF *Florida* COUNTY *Orange*
THE FOREGOING INSTRUMENT WAS ACKNOWLEDGED BEFORE ME THIS *24th* DAY OF *October 2009* BY
Christina Masters ___ WHO ___ IS PERSONALLY KNOWN TO ME OR _X_ HAS PRODUCED *DL M8985746*
AS IDENTIFICATION AND ____ DID TAKE AN OATH _X_ DID NOT TAKE AN OATH.

| *Nancy Notary* | **Nancy Notary** | **10/24/09** | NANCY NOTARY COMMISSION # DO 5555555 EXPIRES: 02/17/2010 |
| NOTARY SIGNATURE | PRINTED NAME | DATE | SEAL |

tion on the jobsite, thereby allowing lienors and others to easily access this information.

It is your responsibility as the homeowner to execute the NOC unless the project is being financed by a construction loan, in which case the lender will execute the document. Lenders often insist on filing the NOC themselves and do not allow work to commence until after the NOC is filed.

Because the NOC is an important legal document, you should be sure that it lists your contact information correctly so that any notices or claims can be properly delivered. Also, you should know that once the Notice of Commencement is filed, construction must begin within a specified time.

Building plans: Your dreams defined

Building plans are the drawings and text that describe the building and its features. Sometimes called "blueprints" because of an earlier printing process that cast a blue color to the paper and lines, the plans are often printed on large sheets of paper that measure approximately 2' x 3'. Today, many drawings are created on a computer using specialized programs that allow draftsmen to work more quickly and thoroughly. Because the drawings are much smaller than the actual structure they represent, they are drawn *to scale*. This establishes a ratio between the drawing and the structure. For example, a drawing may be rendered at ¼ inch to the foot (¼" = 1') so that every ¼-inch increment on the drawing translates to 1 foot in *as built* length. Therefore, a wall measuring 1 inch long on a drawing will measure 4 feet long when constructed. A wall measuring 2 inches high on a drawing will measure 8 feet high when built. You can quickly take measurements from the scale drawings contained in the building plans by using a scale ruler. Because the scale can change throughout a set of plans, each drawing should include a scale notation. For example, a close-up drawing of a specific detail is often rendered in ¾-inch scale (¾" = 1') and must be noted as such.

Depending on the project, the plans may include drawings that show the exterior of the building, called elevations, as well as drawings called the floor plan of the various rooms, their size, and their location. The floor plan will often show the size and location of doors, windows, stairs, bathroom fixtures, kitchen appliances, and cabinets. Lights, outlets, and their circuitry are often shown on a separate sheet, as is the case with plumbing and mechanical systems. Building plans also contain details: detailed drawings of a single component that requires special attention. Although building plans consist primarily of drawings, there may also be several pages of written material that includes general specifications for the project. For example, a specification for fill dirt may require the fill to be free of debris, compacted to 2,500 pounds per square inch (PSI), and chemically treated for termites.

EXAMPLE OF A PLAN DETAIL

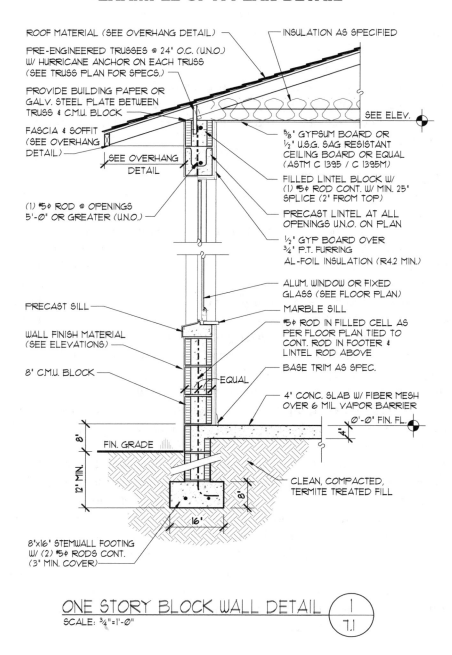

ROOF MATERIAL (SEE OVERHANG DETAIL)

INSULATION AS SPECIFIED

PRE-ENGINEERED TRUSSES @ 24' O.C. (U.N.O.) W/ HURRICANE ANCHOR ON EACH TRUSS (SEE TRUSS PLAN FOR SPECS.)

PROVIDE BUILDING PAPER OR GALV. STEEL PLATE BETWEEN TRUSS & C.M.U. BLOCK

SEE ELEV.

FASCIA & SOFFIT (SEE OVERHANG DETAIL)

SEE OVERHANG DETAIL

⅝" GYPSUM BOARD OR ½" U.S.G. SAG RESISTANT CEILING BOARD OR EQUAL (ASTM C 1395 / C 1395M)

FILLED LINTEL BLOCK W/ (1) #5⌀ ROD CONT. W/ MIN. 25' SPLICE (2' FROM TOP)

(1) #5⌀ ROD @ OPENINGS 5'-0" OR GREATER (U.N.O.)

PRECAST LINTEL AT ALL OPENINGS U.N.O. ON PLAN

½" GYP BOARD OVER ¾" P.T. FURRING AL-FOIL INSULATION (R4.2 MIN.)

ALUM. WINDOW OR FIXED GLASS (SEE FLOOR PLAN)

PRECAST SILL

MARBLE SILL

#5⌀ ROD IN FILLED CELL AS PER FLOOR PLAN TIED TO CONT. ROD IN FOOTER & LINTEL ROD ABOVE

WALL FINISH MATERIAL (SEE ELEVATIONS)

8" C.M.U. BLOCK

EQUAL

BASE TRIM AS SPEC.

4" CONC. SLAB W/ FIBER MESH OVER 6 MIL VAPOR BARRIER

Ø'-Ø" FIN. FL.

8'

FIN. GRADE

12" MIN.

4"

8"

16'

CLEAN, COMPACTED, TERMITE TREATED FILL

8"x16" STEMWALL FOOTING W/ (2) #5⌀ RODS CONT. (3" MIN. COVER)

ONE STORY BLOCK WALL DETAIL
SCALE: ¾"=1'-0"

1

7.1

EXAMPLE OF A FLOOR PLAN AND ELEVATION

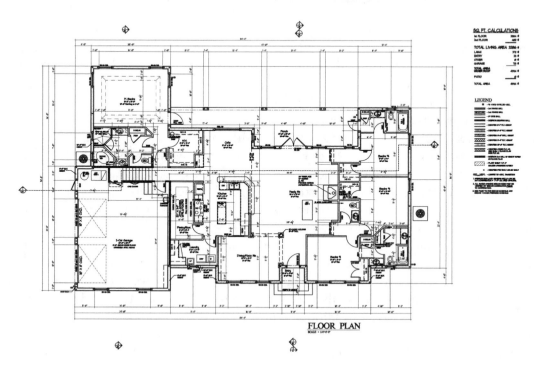

FLOOR PLAN
SCALE = 1/4"=1'-0"

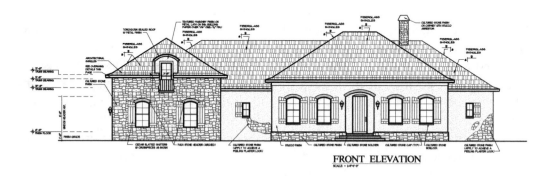

FRONT ELEVATION
SCALE = 1/4"=1'-0"

Design professionals create building plans. In order to create drawings that are acceptable to Building Department authorities, design professionals must be familiar with the building codes and zoning restrictions that affect your project so that your construction documents are in compliance with these standards. Architects are professionally licensed individuals with specialized knowledge in building design. To obtain a license, architects must pass an extensive test about structural, mechanical, plumbing, and electrical systems. They must also be knowledgeable about fire protection systems and site planning, as well as aesthetic design.

To better ensure the success of a project, building plans need to be clear, inclusive, code compliant, and well organized. Otherwise, delays and cost overruns will occur. If the plans contain errors and do not meet building code requirements, the Building Department will reject them. These deficiencies must then be corrected and resubmitted to the Building Department for approval. Not only does this delay the commencement of work, it may also lead to the assessment of additional fees.

More importantly, building plans must contain all the information needed to construct the building. Significant increases in the project cost arise when the plans fail to include all the work you desire and, subsequently, the contractor overlooks these costs when bidding on the project. Only with inclusive plans can a contractor determine the needed work and its cost. In addition, contractors are more productive on the jobsite when building plans are well organized and contain the information they need in order to perform their work. If the plans lack information and are difficult to read, productivity slows—which costs time and money.

Considering these delays and the additional costs, it is often worth hiring an architect to create a good set of plans. It is important to work closely with this professional so that all fixtures (lights, faucets, sinks, toilets, etc.), coverings (carpet, tile, wallpaper, etc.), and appliances are selected before work commences because often these items can be purchased as a package for a better price than when purchased individually. Also, the project will progress in a timely manner if all materials and products are purchased prior to their installation date. People who procrastinate may end up spending more money than is necessary.

Sometimes *stock plans* are purchased from a plans house as a cost-saving alternative to the often more costly plans drafted by architects. Stock plans are pre-drawn plans. In contrast, customized plans are drawings that are created for your specific project. Before purchasing stock plans, it is wise to consider the following questions:

- Does the Building Department require building plans to be stamped by an architect or engineer? If so, does this architect or engineer need to be licensed in the state where the work is to be performed? Do the stock plans

meet this requirement?
- Do the stock plans contain sufficient and accurate code-related information to meet the Building Department's requirements? For example, in Florida, plans must specify the window and door manufacturers and evidence that these items have been approved by the state for windstorm loading (the ability to withstand the physical loads from strong winds). This is critical in areas prone to hurricanes.
- Do the stock plans contain enough detail to enable a contractor to estimate the cost of construction accurately and perform the work efficiently?

If stock plans do not meet these requirements, they can still be used to provide a basic design that can be further revised to meet site conditions, local building codes, and environmental factors such as snow, hurricanes, and earthquakes. The plans house itself can possibly provide these revisions. Otherwise, an architect can make these revisions as long as the modifications do not infringe on copyrights. If the plans require significant revision, inexpensive stock plans may end up costing more than custom plans that are drafted entirely by a licensed architect.

The need for drawings, as well as the level of detail for these drawings, depends on your project and your Building Department's requirements for your project. Whereas the plans documenting the construction of a new home may contain many pages of highly detailed information, some projects, such as the replacement of roofing shingles, may require no plans at all. For information regarding the need for drawings and requirements concerning the drawings' level of detail, contact your municipal Building Department.

The site plan
In addition to providing building plans that show how your structure will be built, it is necessary to show where the construction will occur within the community and within the building lot itself. The site plan is a drawing that shows the building lot, the existing and proposed buildings, adjacent streets, and other features. The applicable department, such as the Zoning, Planning, or Building Department, reviews the site plan to ensure that your project meets standards that reflect the broad vision of the community.

The comprehensive plan: It's the broad vision
It is easy to think that communities just happen—that you simply buy a lot, build a house, and when enough people follow suit, a community is formed. But unlike the past, when a person staked out a homestead, put down a well, and built a house, today's development is a planned affair that requires a broad vision.

EXAMPLE OF A SITE PLAN

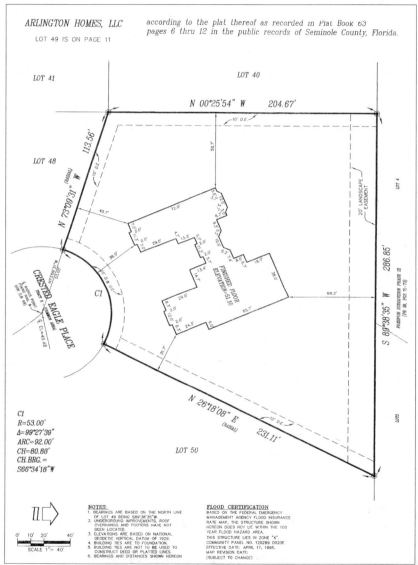

A comprehensive plan comprises guidelines created by the municipal government and community leaders, businesses, and citizens. This plan addresses the needs of the community, as well as future growth and its impact on the environment.

A community requires services such as sewer, water, electricity, gas, police protection, fire protection, education, and transportation. In addition, the community also has recreational, cultural, economic, and housing needs that must be considered. Because these needs are extensive and complex, the community must be arranged in a manner that is functional and efficient. This **urban design** facilitates the intent of a comprehensive plan that provides for the community's requirements.

 Although many consider urban design a recent concept, traces of early urban design exist in ancient cities such as Harappa, which is located in present-day Pakistan. Harappa contained major and minor roadways with symmetrical design, as well as drainage systems for rainwater and sewer. A communal water supply was also available. Ancient Greek and Roman cities also contained urban design elements.

Land use

In order to create a safe, vibrant, and well-functioning community, urban planners must consider how to best use the available land, and the possibilities are many.

Land use designations include broad categories such as residential, commercial, industrial, and agricultural. These categories can be further subdivided into subcategories such as single-family homes, two-family homes, and multiple-family homes, abbreviated as R-1, R-2, and R-3 respectively. Each category has special requirements that address lot size, building height, density, setbacks, use, etc.

EXAMPLE OF POSSIBLE LAND USE DESIGNATIONS

A	Agriculture	MH-2	Mobile Home Park
RE	Single-Family Residential	PUD	Planned Unit Development
R-1	Single-Family Residential	CBD-1	Central Business District 1
R-1A	Single-Family Residential	CBC-2	Central Business District 2
R-1B	Single-Family Residential	NB	Neighborhood Business
R-2A	Single-Family Residential	BC	Business Community
R-2	Single- and Two-Family Residential	P	Professional
		HB	Highway Business
R-3	Multi-Family Residential	I-1	Industrial 1
R-4	Multi-Family Residential	I-2	Industrial 2
MH-A	Mobile Home Annexed	I-2A	Industrial 2A
		I-3	Industrial 3

Variations within a given land use category may be due to slightly differing requirements. For example, an R-1 designation may require the lot size to be a minimum of 10,000 square feet, while a R-1A designation may require a minimum of 15,000 square feet. Other factors, such as building heights, setbacks, etc., may also vary.

In order to achieve compatibility within a community, urban planners assign these land use designations to smaller, independent zones of land so that residential areas are separated from industrial areas, etc. This segregation of land uses into distinct geographic areas with strict use regulations is known as Euclidean zoning, and it has been used extensively because it effectively prevents land use conflicts.

But because of accelerated population growth and the resulting urban sprawl, many planners now design areas that allow mixed use. **Mixed-use developments** integrate schools, shops, parks, and homes within an area that is easily accessible by bike, foot, and public transportation. This recent design movement, which aims to create neighborhoods with diverse uses and inhabitants, is called "new urbanism." But surprisingly, this mixed use is not new at all. Historically, many cities combined commercial and residential uses, not only within a neighborhood, but also within the building itself. These buildings had a business, such as a restaurant or store, on the bottom floor with living quarters above. These mixed-use communities existed because travel was primarily by foot. Therefore, basic provisions needed to be available near the home. Once cars and mass transit became more readily available, residential areas began to develop outside the urban centers in *suburban* areas. This trend created isolated pockets of specific land use.

But as the saying goes, "what goes around comes around." Currently, mixed use is again fashionable because there is an awareness of the environment and the need to preserve it. Mixed-use communities are environmentally friendly because they are walkable, thereby reducing car emissions. Additionally, because mixed-use communities are more densely populated, less land is needed to accommodate the growth that might otherwise sprawl into rural areas. These mixed-use areas, as well as the remaining area that comprises a town, city, or county, are documented on zoning maps that graphically illustrate their allowed land use.

Zoning code

Once a design is created and the land use is determined, the plan needs to be put into force. The zoning code is a tool that legally implements the intent of a comprehensive plan. Many

EXAMPLE OF A ZONING MAP

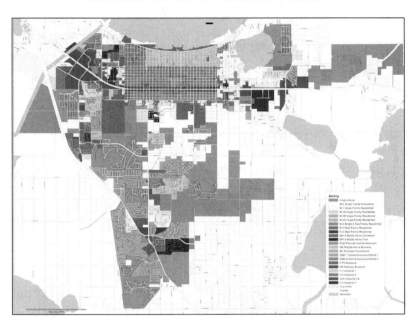

states now call the zoning code the Land Development Code (LDC) because the zoning code, which primarily addresses individual properties, is often incorporated into the LDC. This integration allows the LDC to address the community as a whole.

Most zoning ordinances address the individual properties that make up the community. These ordinances provide for adequate air, light, access, and drainage on your property by regulating the building's size, height, density, and location on the lot. Ordinances restricting height and density may prohibit your neighbor from building a high-rise that blocks your view of a lake or other scenic feature. Ordinances addressing setbacks and easements may prohibit neighbors from building so close to you that you can see what they are eating for dinner.

A *setback* is the distance between the building and the property line that cannot be occupied by the primary structure (e.g., the home). Accessory structures such as sheds, gazebos, and pools may be allowed in the setback area if code allows for this. The setback runs along the perimeter of the property and varies in width from zero to 25 feet in a residentially zoned area. While setbacks do create a feeling of uniformity and openness between buildings, they also have practical purposes, such as providing fire separation, privacy, noise reduction, access, and drainage. Properties in residential areas often have wider setbacks compared to those in commercial areas, which may have no side or rear setbacks at all.

Like setbacks, *easements* are also spaces on a building lot that have limited use. Once the easement is recorded, it transfers some of the rights of land use to the grantee, such as a power company, thereby allowing the company to run power lines through your private property. Your local municipality may secure an easement in order to build a sidewalk or provide for drainage and access. Because these improvements may require maintenance, restrictions may limit what you can place in the easement area. Minor accessories, such as a fence, may be allowed if you agree to remove it at your expense, should it interfere with any work required within the easement. Again, it must also be noted that although the easement is being used by the grantee, you retain the title to this property.

Because setbacks and easements affect the development of your property, they should be shown or described on the site plan.

Flood zones

Floodwater can cause severe damage, especially floodwaters from strong storms that cause rivers to overflow, ground water to rise, and coastal areas to flood due to surging storm water. Because flooding can jeopardize the welfare of a community, the site plan (or separate drainage plan) should demonstrate that a property can successfully shed water. Therefore most site plans are required to show the proposed building pad elevation, the fronting road elevation, and the direction of rainwater flow off the lot. If the property is in a planned community, the property must be graded to tie in with the area's overall drainage design that sends water into the public storm water system and not onto your neighbor's property or onto environmentally sensitive land. Many municipalities require that a licensed surveyor or engineer certify any required site and drainage plans.

 The 100-year flood elevation is determined by analysis of past flood elevations as well as predictive models, and it reflects the maximum height of a flood that has a 1% chance of occurrence in a given year.

Depending on your project, you may also be required to provide an *elevation certificate* if your property is located in a flood zone as determined by the National Flood Insurance Program (NFIP). This certificate verifies whether the building's finished floor elevation is above the 100-year flood elevation. Because floodwaters can have devastating consequences for homeowners, municipalities may prohibit the construction of buildings in flood-prone areas. Development of properties in designated floodways, such as near streams, canals, and creeks, is severely restricted and may require that the structure be placed on piles or posts. The use of fill dirt in these areas is also restricted.

Variances

Similar to the building code, the general intent of zoning code is to create a functional, safe, and healthy community. But on occasion, zoning ordinances may restrict you from using your property. If this is the case, you can apply for a *variance* from an ordinance.

Consider an odd-shaped or very small lot. If the property setbacks prevent, or severely restrict, the size of a house you wish to build, you could request a variance that enables you to encroach into the property setbacks, thereby increasing your buildable land.

Because requests for variances are not uncommon, many municipal governments create a board to review these requests. This board, sometimes called the Board of Adjustments, often consists of officials from the Building, Planning, and Zoning Departments. The Board of Adjustments considers several factors when reviewing a proposed variance. The board reviews site conditions such as the lot size and shape and features such as trees, ponds, and soil. But in addition to physical features of the property, the board must also consider the following:

- Does the existing situation create a hardship that only the variance can remedy?
- Will the variance grant special privileges to the applicant?
- Will the variance harm the public?

Because the public is affected by the board's decision, the community is generally notified of the request for a variance. In many cases, local ordinances address how the public is notified. For example, the property owner, or the Board of Adjustments, may be required to send notices, perhaps via certified mail, to homeowners that live within 200–500 feet of the property that is the subject of the public hearing. Notice of the public hearing may also need to be published in the newspaper. This ensures that the public is made aware of the meeting where they are invited to attend and testify.

Special-use (or conditional-use) permits

When planners assign land use designations to an area, they establish the permitted uses for that land. But in addition to permitted use, they also establish conditional uses. For example, single-family homes are allowed to be built in an area zoned "residential." But churches and other *nonresidential* structures are often built within these residential communities as well. Churches, along with schools, fire stations, and other structures, may be built if planners determine that they are acceptable uses of the land. Therefore, if a church desires to build in a residentially zoned area, a **special-use** or **conditional-use permit** must be issued by the municipality. These permits allow for an exception to the zoning ordinance while preserving the zoning designation. This is much easier than attempting to change the zoning designation to accommodate the proposed change in land use.

As with a request for variance, government officials must review special-use permit applications and consider how the exception will affect the community.

- Will the special use harm the public health or safety?
- Will it adversely affect the value of the adjoining property?
- Is the proposed use in harmony with the surrounding area?

And as with variance requests, the public may also be invited to attend hearings regarding special-use permits.

One more thing about property use

In addition to zoning and building codes, the property may be affected by recorded **conditions, covenants, and restrictions (CCRs)** if it is located in a subdivision or other planned community. CCRs are used to establish a uniform look for an area by establishing standards for building size, building setbacks, color schemes, roofing products, etc. If CCRs are in place, you should review these restrictions with your architect, surveyor, and possibly a competent real estate attorney. Once your building plans are complete, the Home Owner's Association (HOA) and its Architectural Review Committee (ARC) should review the site plan and building plans. It is important to note that these organizations are not affiliated with the municipal government. Therefore, although your building design and your building's location on the lot may be acceptable to the Building and Zoning Departments, you may be in violation of CCRs that affect your property. If that is so, you will be subject to the penalties that the CCRs set forth.

Zoning codes and maps are available at your government offices and may also be available online at the county and city websites. Zoning codes, land development codes, and even government charters from more than 1,600 local governments can be viewed at www.municode.com.

Additional documents for permitting

The documents required for your project depend on the nature of your project and the Building Department's requirements for such projects. If you are building a new house, expect to submit several documents. If you are simply remodeling your kitchen, there will be fewer requirements. The following are examples of documents that may be required for the construction of a new house. Please note that your Building Department may title these documents differently.

Energy calculations provide evidence that the proposed heating and air-conditioning unit can adequately provide sufficient heat and air for your building. The size of the unit is determined through calculations that consider the size of the building and the transfer of (or loss of) heat through windows, doors, floors, walls, and ceilings. Your mechanical contractor, as well as an architect or a mechanical engineer, can provide your energy calculations.

The *engineered truss plan* ensures that the trusses can withstand loads resulting from wind, snow, etc. The truss plan shows the truss design, spacing, and fastening details. The truss supplier, architect, or engineer can provide these drawings and specifications.

The *utility affidavit* provides evidence to the Building Department that electrical service will be available to your building once it has been completed. Affidavits from other service providers, such as trash removal, water, and sewer utilities, may also be necessary. You may be required to establish an account and pay these service providers a fee.

The *address notification form* ensures that a physical street address exists so that emergency responders and other agencies can locate you.

Proof of ownership, in the form of a deed or property tax receipt, etc., is important because it establishes the connection between you—as the homeowner—and your property.

A *subcontractor list* allows the Building Department to check the status of your subcontractors' licenses and their general liability and workers' compensation insurance.

The *owner/builder affidavit* is required if you want to work on your own property and put the permit in your name instead of a contractor's name. Although you do not need to be licensed, you must agree to the restrictions set forth on the affidavit.

Owner/builder permits

Many people consider serving as their own general contractor. Sometimes this works out well; other times the experience is regrettable. Construction can be an exciting process as you watch your dreams become reality. Even a small job that is well done can be a satisfying experience. But an easy undertaking it is not. As this book demonstrates, simply contracting the job is a complicated and time-consuming affair that requires familiarity with construction law and contracts. So much so, that it is often said that the job is half done once you break ground and begin construction.

As discussed earlier, many states require construction work to be performed by licensed and insured contractors because faulty construction can cause harm and illness to the public. Electric, plumbing, and the mechanical trades require licensing in most states. Additionally, a state may require a licensed general contractor to perform structural work and oversee the entire job. By mandating the licensing of contractors, a state helps to ensure these practitioners are competent and ethical.

But many have argued that this requirement restricts homeowners' rights to use their property. In response, many states allow homeowners to obtain a building permit for work on the home they occupy even though they may not meet the state's licensing requirements for contracting. This type of permit is called an owner/builder permit and the owner who obtains it is an owner/builder. In Florida, an owner/builder can build the house from the ground up. Because owner/builders are acting as contractors, they must agree to certain requirements as a condition of permitting. These requirements vary with each Building Department and they may obligate the owner/builder to:

- Occupy the home for one year or longer
- Manage the construction project and not hire an unlicensed construction manager
- Hire licensed contractors for work that is not self-performed or free
- Comply with OSHA regulations
- Comply with workers' compensation regulations
- Comply with building codes
- Withhold employee taxes

The owner/builder may also be restricted to performing work that is under a certain dollar value.

Benefits versus risk

As with most endeavors, there are both benefits and risks associated with assuming the role of general contractor. You may be enticed by the money you may save when acting as

The restriction that requires the owner/builder to occupy a home for a certain amount of time is designed to limit the number of permits he or she may obtain. Without this restriction, an owner/builder might build, or buy and renovate, several homes and sell them— thereby reaping the benefits of a licensed contractor without complying with the state's requirements for this profession.

your own contractor. This sum includes the cost of the general contractor's labor, as well as his overhead and profit. Although this can be a substantial savings, it is only realized if your project does not suffer setbacks from liens, lawsuits, faulty work, and other costly events. People often overlook the fact that licensed contractors are knowledgeable and experienced professionals who meet standards set forth by the state.

When calculating your savings as owner/builder, keep in mind that contractors often purchase materials at a discount. Also, subcontractors may charge less when an experienced general contractor is on board.

What it takes

When a large project is at hand, the duties of a general contractor are numerous and require knowledge and skill to be performed properly. In addition, these duties must often be performed simultaneously, resulting in a juggling act that requires an extraordinary ability to multitask. Therefore before you take on the role of general contractor, you should know the duties that will be required of you. Your duties as general contractor may include:

- Interpreting the building plans and defining the entire scope of work
- Estimating material and labor costs
- Selecting subcontractors and verifying licensing and insurance documents
- Obtaining subcontractor proposals
- Executing contracts with the subcontractors
- Obtaining building permits for the job
- Ordering materials and scheduling delivery
- Scheduling subcontractors
- Supervising subcontractors while on site
- Ensuring jobsite safety
- Inspecting the work for accuracy and code compliancy
- Scheduling and overseeing inspections

- Paying subcontractors and suppliers
- Managing lien releases

If you assume the role of general contractor without experience and knowledge, and the project is of a significant size, you may find that it exceeds your capability. As a result, you may lose any savings that you hoped to retain by not having a general contractor on board.

It is a frequent practice of CONtractors to ask an owner to obtain an owner/builder permit. Beware!

Owner/builder failure

Owner/builders are often surprised by the difficulties they encounter during construction, especially on large projects that require multiple subcontractors. Subsequently, many owner/builders fall short because they do not know what to do, and when to do it.

Before you undertake a challenging project, you should have some knowledge of the various construction trades. Although licensed subcontractors are skilled tradesmen whose work is inspected by Building Department officials when a permit is in place, you will still be called upon to make decisions during the construction process. Sometimes building plans conflict with existing conditions and a change must be made. This changed work may also affect the work that follows it. To make an informed and timely decision, you must have a basic understanding of construction.

Correctly scheduling the various trades is also a challenging procedure if you are unfamiliar with the construction process. The finished product depends on the proper sequence of construction events. Sometimes a scheduling error may have only minor consequences. For example, if the worksite or materials are unavailable, a subcontractor may have to return at a later date. If there is a cost for this inconvenience, it is generally insignificant. But scheduling errors can be costly. Consider the expense of a foundation that is poured before the soil is properly prepared. To provide adequate support for a foundation, the soil must be free of debris, compacted, treated for termites, and at the proper elevation. If this is overlooked, the cost to repair this mistake is great indeed because the foundation would likely have to be demolished and re-poured. Although building inspections often prevent these kinds of catastrophic errors, mistakes of this magnitude do occur.

Underestimating estimating

Estimating the cost of a large project challenges many contractors, let alone someone without construction knowledge. If you do not know what steps are required, how do you allow for this cost? But this is not the only challenge. Once you have identified the steps, you need to correctly estimate their cost. To do this, you must be able to interpret the building plans and perform complex calculations.

Measurements require the use of scale rulers and other instruments. This data must then be manipulated to provide answers. Therefore, you must also know what mathematical formula will provide the information you need. Although building plans provide the information necessary to perform a calculation, the plans do not provide the mathematical formulas. Area, volume, and distance calculations result from specific formulas—and when the wrong formula is used, the wrong answer will result. If material quantities are calculated incorrectly, the estimated cost for these materials will also be incorrect.

Time ... is not on your side

Many owner/builders underestimate the amount of time required to effectively perform their role as contractor. For you to be a successful owner/builder, you must play an active role, start to finish. This includes providing leadership and guidance during the construction phase. Your availability during the workday is essential to a project's timely success because questions arise and must be answered. Nothing goes entirely as planned. Sometimes unknown conditions become evident during construction; these conditions alter the planned course of action. Other times, building plans require clarification. Communication is essential to the success of any project and takes place throughout the day during the entire course of the construction process.

If you undertake a large construction project as owner/builder, be prepared to spend a significant amount of time on your jobsite. The complexity of your project and the quality of the building plans will determine how much time this will be. If you have a full-time job, you may find that you cannot effectively oversee your project. This may compromise both your project and your job! Surely your boss will not be pleased if you spend a large part of your day on the phone with your subcontractors. And if you put off the subcontractors' questions, they may leave for another jobsite, thereby delaying your job and possibly increasing your job cost if they charge you a return trip fee.

If you obtain an owner/builder permit and lack the knowledge and time to perform your duties, you should consider hiring a construction manager to oversee construction.

In fact, it may be required. Florida, for example, requires an owner/builder to directly supervise the work or hire a person who is licensed in the trade that he or she is overseeing. Many construction managers are licensed contractors and their licensing may be a requirement of the owner/builder permit.

A look at liability

Another very important issue to consider as owner/builder is liability. When you obtain an owner/builder permit, you take on the liabilities that would otherwise be the contractor's. As owner/builder you are personally responsible for supervision, performance, safety, and the payment of any required taxes. Did you know that if you pay an unlicensed and uninsured contractor (let's call him Jeff Davis) in contrast to a company (Jeff Davis Carpenters, Inc., for example), you may be considered an employer under state and federal law? As an employer, you may be responsible for payroll taxes, unemployment compensation, and workers' compensation. If you fail to meet your obligations and you are caught, you may owe fines in addition to the money owed. Criminal penalties may also be imposed.

Because the duties and responsibilities of owner/builder are significant, many Building Departments require the owner to sign an affidavit that delineates these duties. In Florida, owners who apply for an owner/builder permit must acknowledge the following statement (or similar language):

DISCLOSURE STATEMENT

State law requires construction to be done by licensed contractors. You have applied for a permit under an exemption to that law. The exemption allows you, as the owner of your property, to act as your own contractor with certain restrictions even though you do not have a license. You must provide direct, onsite supervision of the construction yourself. You may build or improve a one-family or two-family residence or a farm outbuilding. You may also build or improve a commercial building, provided your costs do not exceed $25,000. The building or residence must be for your own use or occupancy. It may not be built or substantially improved for sale or lease. If you sell or lease a building you have built or substantially improved yourself within one year after the construction is complete, the law will presume that you built or substantially improved it for sale or lease, which is a violation of this exemption. You may not hire an unlicensed person to act as your contractor *or to supervise people working on your building. It is your responsibility to make sure that people employed by you have licenses required by state law and by county or municipal licensing ordinances. You may not delegate the responsibility for supervising work to a licensed contractor who is not licensed to perform the work being done. Any person working on your building who is not licensed must work under your direct supervision and must be employed by you, which means that you must deduct FICA and withholding tax and provide workers' compensation for that employee, all as prescribed by law. Your construction must comply with all applicable laws, ordinances, building codes, and zoning regulations.*

Often, this type of affidavit further clarifies the liabilities of owner/builder. For example, the affidavit may include the following statement:

"I understand that I am legally and financially responsible for proposed construction activity and I agree that, as the party legally and financially responsible for this proposed construction activity, I will abide by all the applicable laws and requirements that govern owner/builders and employers."

If you are an employer, failure to secure workers' compensation insurance is unlawful and may subject you to criminal penalties and civil fines in addition to the cost of premiums, compensation, and damages.

Look before you leap

Before you step into the contractor's shoes and act as owner/builder, be aware that these may be big shoes to fill. A contractor's duties are numerous and require time and knowledge to be performed effectively. In addition, consider the liability that you assume when a permit is issued in your name. ***There can be serious consequences for the owner/ builder who is unprepared and unqualified to assume the responsibilities of construction contracting.*** Although many people have successfully performed as an owner/builder, particularly those with construction experience who undertake small- to medium-sized jobs, many first-time owner/builders have found that the work was not worth the money saved. Before you obtain an owner/builder permit, consider the amount of work and liability involved compared to the cost of the general contractor, who generally charges between 15% and 20% of the project cost.

Financing your project with a lender may be difficult or impossible if you are an owner/builder because owner/builders frequently fail to complete their projects on budget.

Permitting questions and process

Once the Building Department accepts your permitting package for review, a permit number will be issued. Many Building Departments maintain a website that allows you to track the status of your project as it is reviewed by the various departments. Otherwise, the Building Department will most likely contact you once the project review is complete.

Missing or incorrect information is often flagged by various departments and must be corrected as a condition for approval. It is best to anticipate possible errors and allow time to both revise and resubmit the construction documents for review. During this review process, the Building Department may authorize an "early start permit" that allows you to begin preliminary work such as site and foundation preparation. But be aware that if the Building Department rejects your project entirely, this early work may be a costly and wasted effort.

Once the project is approved and the plans reviewed, impact fees may be due. These amounts vary with each municipality and can be a significant expense in urban areas where impact fees help pay for public services such as transportation, education, and fire protection.

Once the permit is issued, laws often stipulate that the work must commence within a certain amount of time, such as six months, or the permit becomes void. During construction, the Notice of Commencement, the permitted plans, the building permit, and inspection card (if a separate document) must be kept on the jobsite—and the accessibility of these documents is often a prerequisite of the first inspection.

12
INSPECTIONS:
GET THEM DONE RIGHT

Whew! As you can see, the pre-construction effort is intensive and yet you have little physical evidence of your work. But once your building documents are approved, your permit will be issued and work is authorized to proceed. The permit should include a list of inspections that are required by the Building Department. Whereas a simple repair job may require only a final inspection, the construction of a new house will require several inspections. The appropriate inspector from the Building Department performs these inspections. For example, the *building inspector* focuses on the structural aspects of a building whereas an *electrical inspector* reviews the electrical system. Plumbing and mechanical inspectors also have specialized training in their fields. The various inspectors share one common goal: to ensure that your work is done per plan and in compliance with building codes.

Building codes
Building codes are standards that help to protect the public's health, safety, and general well-being. These codes not only address the structural integrity of a building, but also set forth standards for the building's components and systems, such as electrical, heat and air, etc.

Building codes safeguard the public and promote well-being by creating standards for:
- Structural strength
- Sanitation
- Light and ventilation
- Energy conservation
- Fire protection
- Egress (means of exit)
- Handicap access

The history of building codes

Although buildings have evolved from primitive structures to complex works of art, a perfect structure has yet to be built. Flawed building materials and methods continuously challenge engineers, contractors, and other professionals who seek to remedy the damage that faulty materials and methods can cause. But this effort is not a new one. The danger from flawed construction was recognized and addressed by law in early history.

In 1760 B.C., the Babylonian King Hammurabi created a code of laws that was inscribed on a stone pillar. In addition to laws about agriculture, livestock, laborers, slaves, marriage, divorce, inheritance, sales, perjury, theft, debt, etc., the Code of Hammurabi also established laws about construction. These laws reveal not only that the building trade was well established at the time, but also that faulty construction was recognized as harmful. The following excerpt from the Code of Hammurabi contains construction-related laws that may be some of the earliest building codes:

228. If a builder builds a house for someone and completes it, he shall give him a fee of two shekels in money for each sar of surface.

229. If a builder builds a house for someone, and does not construct it properly, and the house which he built falls in and kills its owner, then that builder shall be put to death.

230. If it kills the son of the owner, the son of that builder shall be put to death.

231. If it kills a slave of the owner, then he shall pay slave for slave to the owner of the house.

232. If it ruins goods, he shall make compensation for all that has been ruined, in as much as he did not construct properly this house which he built and it fell, he shall re-erect the house from his own means.

233. If a builder builds a house for someone, and even though he has not yet completed it, if the wall seems to be toppling, the builder must make the walls solid from his own means.

This "eye for an eye" style of punishment was spelled out literally in the Code of Hammurabi: "196. If a man puts out the eye of another man, his eye shall be put out."

Faulty construction was not the only cause of building-related catastrophes. Fire has also devastated communities throughout history. In 1666, the Great Fire of London destroyed more than 13,000 buildings that housed up to 90% of the population. This fire and others revealed the hazards of using combustible building materials such as wood and straw, especially in large cities with minimal space between the buildings.

Although wood is combustible, it continues to be a popular building material because it is strong, lightweight, and readily available.

In the 1700s, Benjamin Franklin studied building materials and methods with the goal of eliminating fires in buildings. He advocated the use of plaster as a non-combustible material that could be used to slow the spread of fire. He also prescribed acceptable clearances of combustible materials, particularly in areas adjacent to the fireplace. In one of his correspondences, he wrote: "None of the wooden work communicates with the wooden work of any other room." One of his most famous inventions, the lightning rod, helped prevent fire caused by lightning. Franklin speculated that "The electrical fire would, I think, be drawn out of a cloud silently, before it could come near enough to strike." Benjamin Franklin's discoveries are noteworthy and they are incorporated into our modern building code.

After a visit to Boston, Benjamin Franklin urged the citizens of Philadelphia to form a fire department that would meet regularly, practice, and attend all fires. He also suggested that chimney sweeps should be licensed and be held accountable for their work.

Building codes today

Recently, building codes and the organizations that develop them underwent a significant transformation. Prior to 1994, these building code councils were regional and maintained their own sets of codes. Because of the desire to create a comprehensive **model code** without regional limitations, a single code entity, the International Code Council (ICC), was created.

The ICC comprises code officers, contractors, engineers, design professionals, trade associations, suppliers, manufacturers, governmental agencies, and anyone with an interest in building codes. The ICC meets regularly to review and develop building codes. Once the codes are approved, they are adopted by most states and then modified to accommodate special conditions such as snow, ice, rain, wind, high water, sun, sand, muck, salt, and seismic activity. As a result, Florida's building code contains provisions that address hurricane winds while California's code provides for conditions that occur during earthquakes.

In addition to changes in the codes at state level, local government may have the ability to further modify building codes if stricter standards are needed. For example, buildings occupying Florida's coastline have stricter code requirements than buildings located in the interior of the state because the coast is exposed to higher winds during hurricanes. As a result, roofing materials used on coastal properties may require additional fasteners. Other modifications are necessary as well.

Not all building types are subject to building code compliance. Exemptions may include federally owned buildings, Indian tribe buildings, farm structures, storage sheds, and temporary construction buildings.

Before you schedule

An inspection can be easily scheduled by phone, fax, and possibly online by you, your contractor, or your representatives. Before scheduling an inspection, be sure to know the permit number, jobsite address, and the type of inspection you want. Once the inspection is scheduled, ensure that the jobsite and work item that is to be inspected are accessible to the inspector. Unlock any gates and doors so that the inspector can enter the jobsite, and place the plans and permit in plain view where the inspector has ready access to them.

Meet the inspector

There are many instances in life when a small gesture makes a big difference. Meeting your building inspector is one example of this. It is highly recommended that you, your

EXAMPLE OF AN INSPECTION LIST

MY COUNTY BUILDING DEPARTMENT
12 BUSINESS SQUARE
SUITE 260
ANYTOWN, FL 55583
(555) 555-1756

INSPECTION REQUEST LINE: (555) 555-1757

PERMIT # **09-1768**
DATE: **11-30-2009**
CONTRACTOR/OWNER: **IMA Contractor Inc.**
JOB SITE ADDRESS: **2526 Tyson Road Anytown, FL 55583**

INSPECTION ACCESS CODE: **4114**

BUILDING INSPECTIONS
1000 FOOTINGS/FOUNDATION
1010 SLAB
1100 LINTEL/TIE BEAM/DOWN CELL
1200 FRAMING INCLUDING STRAPPING
1300 EXTERIOR SHEATHING/STRAPPING
1400 FIRES TOPPING
1500 INSULATION
1600 DRYWALL SCREW (COMMERCIAL ONLY)
1610 DRYWALL FINAL (COMMERCIAL ONLY)
1700 BUILDING — OTHER
1800 BUILDING — FINAL

ELECTRICAL INSPECTIONS
2000 TEMPORARY POWER POLE
2010 TEMPORARY UNDERGROUND
2100 ELECTRICAL — UNDERGROUND
2200 ELECTRICAL ROUGH
2300 ELECTRICAL WALL AND CEILINGS
2400 ELECTRICAL SERVICE UPGRADE
2500 ELECTRICAL — OTHER
2600 PRE POWER
2700 ELECTRICAL FINAL

PLUMBING INSPECTIONS
3000 UNDERGROUND
3100 PLUMBING ROUGH
3200 TUB SET
3400 PLUMBING — OTHER
3500 PLUMBING FINAL

GAS INSPECTIONS
4000 GAS ROUGH
4100 GAS FINAL

MECHANICAL INSPECTIONS
5000 MECHANICAL ROUGH
5100 MECHANICAL — OTHER
5200 MECHANICAL — FINAL

ROOF INSPECTIONS
6000 SHEATHING
6100 DRY-IN AND FLASHING
6200 ROOF-FINAL

POOL INSPECTIONS
7000 STEEL AND GROUNDING
7100 DECK AND PRESSURE PIPING TEST
7200 POOL — FINAL

MISC. INSPECTIONS
8000 FENCE FINAL
8100 WINDOW/DOOR REPLACEMENT FINAL
8200 DEMOLITION
8300 SCREEN FINAL
8400 LANDSCAPING
8500 IRRIGATION
8600 MISCELLANEOUS

contractor, or your representative be on site when the inspector arrives so that work issues can be more quickly resolved. For example, an inspector may have a question or comment about the work and this matter is often more easily discussed than written as a report. Additionally, an inspector can directly point out the exact location of the deficient work to someone on the jobsite. You should also consider this: By being present during an inspection, you can discuss a course of action that is acceptable to both you and the inspector. If only a minor correction is needed, you may be able to do it quickly while the inspector is on site.

In contrast, if no one can meet with the inspector, the inspector must write this information on the jobsite inspection card or online report (if your Building Department provides this service). The information may be limited to only the building code section number and a brief explanation of the violation. Once the violation is noted, the deficient work must often be corrected and re-inspected before you are allowed to schedule additional inspections. If other work continues before the needed corrections are made, a Building Department official may issue a stop-work order.

R-E-S-P-E-C-T

Another small gesture that may influence your project outcome is respect. It is important to give inspectors the respect and courtesy that their position deserves. These individuals are often state-licensed professionals who must obtain a license based on technical knowledge, experience, and education. Additionally, many states require that these officials pass an exam on topics such as building codes, construction methods and materials, and ethics. Because building codes change, continuing education is often required of building inspectors. This training broadens and updates an inspector's knowledge.

Inspections may be performed by registered architects and engineers if your Building Department allows for this.

A quick look at inspections

In order for a house to be a safe and healthy environment, it must be structurally sound and free from defects that can cause fire, flood, and other hazards. Therefore the inspector enforces building codes intended to prevent these unwanted events. Much of the work toward code compliancy is accomplished when the building plans are reviewed for permitting. If a house is built using the approved plans, then it generally will comply with code. But because plans don't always contain every detail about construction, contractors rely on their trade knowledge to perform this work. The inspector must verify that this work, as well as all remaining work, complies with code. Additionally, the inspector must verify that all required activities, such as surveying and soil testing, have been performed and documented.

From the bottom up

The number of inspections that will be required for your project will depend on the nature of your project and your Building Department's requirements for that type of project. When a new house is built, the "foundation inspection" typically occurs first. This often requires a foundation survey that notes the foundation's location and height. A foundation survey helps to ensure that the foundation is built in the right place and at the correct elevation.

Because the foundation has the important job of supporting the house, many of the inspected items are structural in nature. Rebar is critical to the foundation's ability to support loads because rebar increases concrete's strength. Therefore the inspector looks at rebar placement and size within the foundation.

 Although concrete has high compression strength that allows heavy loads to bear directly down on it, concrete readily fractures when it is bent and in tension. *For example, concrete's compressive strength often reaches 3,000 pounds per square inch (psi) but* its tensile strength may be only 54 psi.

Because the footer, that is, the thickened edge of the foundation, is where most of the load is transferred, an inspector will make sure the footer dimensions are per the approved plans. But it must be noted that a properly constructed foundation is of little use if the soil beneath it is poor or improperly prepared.

The soil building pad must be free of debris that can compromise the pad's ability to support loads placed on it. Organic debris such as wood can rot, thereby allowing soil to shift. This in turn may cause the concrete foundation to crack. Therefore, clean soil must be used under a foundation and it must also be compacted to the density specified by code. Soil density tests are performed by engineers and the results are often required by the building inspector. A termite treatment certificate, which verifies that the soil has been treated for termites, is also often required. These issues and more are addressed by the inspector during the foundation inspection before the concrete is poured.

If the walls could talk ...

... They would tell you that they are typically constructed with concrete, concrete block, or wood. Solid concrete walls and walls built with concrete block also use rebar to increase structural strength. Therefore, inspectors look at rebar size and placement within these walls. Concrete and concrete block work over doors and windows must be properly constructed in order to be strong enough to span these openings. Walls constructed with wood also require properly constructed door and window openings. Metal fasteners are used in all wall systems to create a secure connection to the trusses above and the floors below.

The inspector also reviews the roof system that completes the **building envelope**. Elements such as wind and snow place significant loads on the roof. Therefore the roof must be properly constructed to withstand these loads. If the roof is constructed with wood, the wood sheathing must be nailed securely to the trusses. Roofing materials such as shingles must be correctly installed so that the roof is weather tight. Siding must also be weather tight.

The inspector also has the important job of ensuring that electrical, plumbing, and HVAC (heating, ventilating, and air conditioning) systems are to code. Properly sized pipes, wires, and ducts are essential to a well-functioning system. Because pipes and wires often run through walls, they must be protected from nails that might accidently penetrate them when drywall is installed. Holes in the wood where pipes and wires travel must be of minimal size so that the structural integrity of the wood is not compromised. Since electric, plumbing, and HVAC are specialized trades, specially trained inspectors may be responsible for inspecting these components of your building project.

Drywall, insulation, windows, and doors finalize the building envelope and must be installed per code to ensure that the building is weather tight. Doors and windows that are installed in homes built in areas prone to hurricanes have special requirements. Not only must the products meet the code requirements for high wind, these products also must be properly installed so that they are not dislodged during a storm.

The home stretch

The last inspection in the inspection series is the final building inspection. This is made after all required inspections, such as the final mechanical, electrical, plumbing, and gas inspections, are performed and approved.

Because several inspections are usually performed during the construction of a new home, the final building inspection addresses issues not yet approved during earlier inspections. This may include a review of the following:

- Smoke detectors are hardwired and interconnected with battery backup.
- Appliances and fixtures are in place.
- Floor finishes and trim are level, flush, and without gaps.
- Pipe penetrations are caulked.
- Windows and doors are weather tight.
- Electrical systems are energized with fixtures in place.
- Sewer and water service is operational with plumbing fixtures in place.
- Lot grade sheds water away from house; no soil within 6 inches of exterior siding, stucco, etc.
- Street number, usually 3-inches tall, is legible from the street.

Prior to approval, final reports from engineers and surveyors may also be needed, as well as approval from the fire marshal if required. Once all the required paperwork and inspections are approved, the building may be occupied. This approval is made official by the issuance of a Certificate of Occupancy (CO) or a Certificate of Completion (CC).

The Certificate of Occupancy is an official document issued by the Building Department when a building satisfies the building code's requirements for occupancy. A CO is issued for new structures and may include additions and buildings where a change of use has occurred (such as a change from residential to commercial use).

The Certificate of Completion is issued for projects that have already been certified for occupation. For example, a CC may be issued for a remodel or addition. A CC may also be issued for swimming pools. This official document is issued by the Building Department once the requirements for the completed structure are met.

It is important to know that the issuance of a CO or CC does not guarantee that the work is completely finished. For example, the painted trim may require touch-up. This minor deficiency does not create a condition that renders the structure unready to be occupied. To ensure that these minor deficiencies are corrected, the contract must provide for this by allowing for a punch list of deficiencies that will be corrected by the contractor.

Inspection = protection

Building codes safeguard the public's safety, health, and well-being. Prior to commencing work, the Building Department reviews your construction documents, such as the building plans, to ensure that they comply with these codes. Once approved, a building permit is issued and work may begin.

A building permit is an agreement between you (who agrees to perform work that is code compliant) and the Building Department (who agrees to inspect the work for code compliancy). The building inspector is the Building Department's representative who inspects your work for code compliancy.

Because construction is often a complex task, teamwork is essential to a successful outcome. Frequent communication with the Building Department and building inspector will ensure that you are informed of the requirements for your job. Through a respectful and communicative relationship with them, your common goal—the successful completion of your project—is more readily accomplished.

A LOOK AT LIENS

Construction is an exciting undertaking and it should be a smooth one if your construction documents are inclusive and clear. But unfortunately, even the best laid plans can go awry. Benjamin Franklin wrote that "nothing is certain but death and taxes." Many would add that disagreements are also certain to occur. In construction, these disagreements often involve money—more specifically, money owed.

As discussed earlier, money is generally exchanged for the work, materials, and supplies provided by your contractor. If a disagreement occurs regarding nonpayment for services rendered, a ***claim of lien*** may result. Construction lien laws are some of the most important laws that affect property owners who undertake a construction project. Unfortunately, many owners are unfamiliar with these laws even though they may have to pay twice or risk losing their property as a result of these liens.

Promises, promises

Collateral has long been used to secure debts, especially when the debt is great. Consider, for example, a mortgage. When you borrow money to buy a house, the bank holds the title until the debt is paid. Why? Because when collateral secures a debt, the stakes are higher and the debt is likely to be paid. As the saying goes, "you have a horse in the race."

One unusual aspect of the construction industry is an unpaid contractor's or supplier's ability to secure a debt by recording a claim of lien on the property where the work was performed. When a claim of lien is recorded, the property becomes collateral until the matter is settled.

Holy hostage, Batman

Liens and lienors

A claim of lien is a recorded document that secures a debt owed to a "lienor"—an unpaid contractor or supplier who is "eligible" to claim a lien per state law. Depending on which state you live in, lienors can include general contractors, architects, subcontractors, sub-subcontractors, laborers, and material suppliers. Again, because the word "lienor" can readily be misunderstood as only those who claim a lien, it must be emphasized that lienors also include anyone who is *eligible* to claim a lien per state law. It does not mean that the lienor will do so.

When a claim of lien is placed on a property, there are serious consequences. First, a claim of lien clouds the title of a property. As a result, the title is no longer "clean" and easily transferred. This creates problems for both buyers and sellers. For example, perhaps you want to sell your property. If there is a claim of lien attached to your title, the buyer may not be able to get financing until the claimed amount is paid (or dismissed by other means). But there is much more at stake than the possible problems with financing.

Lien laws also contain provisions that may force you to sell your property with the money from the sale going toward payment of the lien amount.

Foreclosure sales

Unless you have been directly affected by lien law, it is easy to underestimate its power. Lienors that file a claim of lien can take legal action (more specifically, file a lawsuit to foreclose) that may force you to sell your property. This is significant when you consider that in Florida, for example, there are generally only three instances in which you can be forced to sell your permanent residence (i.e., homestead): They are when:

1. Federal, state, or local taxes are owed.
2. Your mortgage goes unpaid.
3. Improvements or repairs of the homestead go unpaid and a lien is filed and awarded.

Therefore, your unpaid plumber shares some of the same powers as the IRS and banks. This may seem unfair, especially if you must pay twice to settle the claim of lien.

Unfair?

Laws often create controversy because sometimes they benefit one party at the expense of another. States that enacted lien law felt the need to protect the interests of lienors who improve a property and are not paid. Lienors extend thousands of dollars in credit to property owners by providing materials and labor to the jobsite before getting paid. If this debt goes unpaid, it is highly unlikely that these lienors will be able to recover their material and labor costs. The lumber is nailed in the wall. Plumbing pipes are cut, glued, and buried deep in the ground. In fact, law may prevent them from repossessing these items. Therefore lien laws help to ensure that lienors are paid, even though it may come at a cost to you.

An alarming aspect of lien law is that ***you may be forced to pay twice to settle the claim of lien***. For example, your property could become subject to a claim of lien even when you paid the general contractor whose duty it is to pay the subcontractors and suppliers. If the general contractor did not pay them, lien laws may require you to pay these lienors in order to prevent or satisfy a claim of lien. That means you pay twice, once to the general contractor and again to the subcontractor or supplier who improved your property. Therefore it is important to take action to avoid claims of lien from occurring altogether.

Know thy lienors

Because a claim of lien can have serious consequences, lien laws contain provisions that protect you against claims of lien. But this protection requires you to obtain specific documents from your lienors. Before you can do this, you need to know who these lienors are. Each state's lien laws have provisions that address who has lien rights. This information is contained in your state's statutes, which can be readily accessed online.

 To ensure you reach the state website, use search words such as "state of Florida statutes." Once you arrive at the website (which will most likely contain the domain ".gov" or ".us"), look for a search function and enter search words such as "construction lien," "lienor," and "claim of lien." This list of returns should provide you with the statutes relevant to your search.

In Florida, and several other states, lienors are generally divided into three tiers as follows:

- The first tier consists of lienors in direct contract with you, such as the general contractor.
- The second tier consists of lienors that are not in direct contract with you because they are hired by the general contractor. They may include subcontractors and their material suppliers.
- The third tier consists of lienors that are not in direct contract with you because they are hired by a subcontractor. They include sub-subcontractors and their material suppliers.

A sub-subcontractor is a contractor hired by a subcontractor to perform a specialized trade. For example, a general contractor (often called a "prime contractor"—first tier) hires an electrician (a subcontractor—second tier) who in turn hires an alarm company (a sub-subcontractor—third tier) to install the security system in a house. In Florida, this sub-subcontractor has lien rights. So does his or her material supplier. Other states may not grant lien rights to sub-subcontractors or their suppliers.

Once you have identified which entities have lien rights in your state, you now need to determine which specific entities have lien rights on your project. This is a relatively easy task if you contracted with them directly because you know who most of these lienors are. But if you hire a general contractor—who in turn hires subcontractors—you may not know the lienors. In this instance, you must obtain a list of lienors from the general contractor, *who may be required by law* to provide this information to you. In Florida, the lien statute reads: "An owner of real property may request from the contractor a list of all subcontractors and suppliers who have any contract with the contractor." Note that this request must be in writing and delivered by registered or certified mail to the address of the contractor as shown on the contract or Notice of Commencement. If the contractor fails to furnish this list within 10 days, the contractor may lose some of his lien rights.

There are also other provisions in lien law that will help you identify your lienors.

 Because identifying sub-subcontractors is complicated and time consuming, many general contractors avoid this matter entirely by forbidding their subcontractors from hiring other subcontractors. This condition is written into the general contractor's contract with each subcontractor. As a result, any sub-subcontractor must contract directly with the general contractor, thereby making him or her a subcontractor.

Lienor's duties under lien law

One of the foremost duties of a lienor who wants to preserve the right to file a claim of lien is to let you know that he or she is improving your property.

A Notice to Owner (NTO) is a document that notifies you that a particular lienor has furnished labor, services, or materials to improve your property. Because you may not know this lienor, the Notice to Owner might be considered a letter of introduction. The information conveyed goes like this:

"Hello Owner, my name is John from IMA Plumber, Inc., and I have been contracted to improve your property. Please make sure that I am paid so that I do not have to place a lien on your property."

EXAMPLE OF A NOTICE TO OWNER

Owner: Dottie Smith
General Contractor: New Home Production, Inc.
Subcontractor: IMA Plumber, Inc.

WARNING! FLORIDA'S CONSTRUCTION LIEN LAW ALLOWS SOME UNPAID CONTRACTORS, SUBCONTRACTORS, AND MATERIAL SUPPLIERS TO FILE LIENS AGAINST YOUR PROPERTY EVEN IF YOU HAVE MADE PAYMENT IN FULL. UNDER FLORIDA LAW, YOUR FAILURE TO MAKE SURE THAT WE ARE PAID MAY RESULT IN A LIEN AGAINST YOUR PROPERTY AND YOUR PAYING TWICE. TO AVOID A LIEN AND PAYING TWICE, YOU MUST OBTAIN A WRITTEN RELEASE FROM US EVERY TIME YOU PAY YOUR CONTRACTOR.

NOTICE TO OWNER

TO: **Dottie Smith 2020 New Homes Way, Anytown, FL 55584**
DATE: **May 15, 2009**

THE UNDERSIGNED HEREBY INFORMS YOU THAT HE/SHE HAS FURNISHED OR IS FURNISHING SERVICES OR MATERIALS AS FOLLOWS: (GENERAL DESCRIPTION OF LABOR, SERVICES OR MATERIALS) **IMA Plumber, Inc. has provided plumbing supplies and services for all plumbing requirements per Sheet P-1 Smith Residential Home dated: March 7, 2009** FOR THE IMPROVEMENT OF THE REAL PROPERTY IDENTIFIED AS: (PROPERTY DESCRIPTION) **2020 New Homes Way Anytown, FL 55584 (WEST LAKE ESTATE UNIT 2 PB 2 PG 108 LOT 29 09-26-30)**

UNDER AN ORDER GIVEN BY: (NAME OF THE PERSON WHO CONTRACTED WITH THE UNDERSIGNED) **New Home Production, Inc. c/o Tom Builder, President 2578 Pine Tree Way Anytown, FL 55582**

FLORIDA LAW PRESCRIBES THE SERVICING OF THIS NOTICE AND RESTRICTS YOUR RIGHT TO MAKE PAYMENTS UNDER YOUR CONTRACT IN ACCORDANCE WITH SECTION 713.06, FLORIDA STATUTES.

IMPORTANT INFORMATION FOR YOUR PROTECTION:
UNDER FLORIDA'S LAWS, THOSE WHO WORK ON YOUR PROPERTY OR PROVIDE MATERIALS AND ARE NOT PAID, HAVE A RIGHT TO ENFORCE THEIR CLAIM FOR PAYMENT AGAINST YOUR PROPERTY. THIS CLAIM IS KNOWN AS A CONSTRUCTION LIEN. IF YOUR CONTRACTOR FAILS TO PAY SUBCONTRACTORS OR MATERIAL SUPPLIERS OR NEGLECTS TO MAKE OTHER LEGALLY REQUIRED PAYMENTS, THE PEOPLE WHO ARE OWED MONEY MAY LOOK TO YOUR PROPERTY FOR PAYMENT, EVEN IF YOU HAVE PAID YOUR CONTRACTOR IN FULL.

PROTECT YOURSELF
RECOGNIZE THAT THIS NOTICE TO OWNER MAY RESULT IN A LIEN AGAINST YOUR PROPERTY UNLESS ALL THOSE SUPPLYING A NOTICE TO OWNER HAVE BEEN PAID. LEARN MORE ABOUT THE CONSTRUCTION LIEN LAW, CHAPTER 713, PART 1, FLORIDA STATUTES, AND THE MEANING OF THIS NOTICE BY CONTACTING AN ATTORNEY OR THE FLORIDA DEPARTMENT OF BUSINESS AND PROFESSIONAL REGULATION.

BY: (LIENOR) **John Hancock — President**
LIENOR'S SIGNATURE: *John Hancock*
COMPANY: **IMA Plumber, Inc.**
ADDRESS: **123 Main St. Anytown, FL 55584**

COPIES TO: **New Home Production, Inc**
           Loaded Lenders

You may also receive an NTO from John's plumbing supply company if it is eligible to claim lien and wants to retain the right to do so. In this regard, the NTO is especially helpful because it lets you know of lienors that are far removed from you, such as suppliers and sub-subcontractors. But keep in mind that the NTO is more than a means of introduction. By sending an NTO, lienors have taken a necessary step toward securing their right to record a claim of lien. This does not necessarily mean that they will claim a lien, but instead that they want to preserve the right to claim a lien. Like a train ticket, just because they bought one doesn't mean they are necessarily taking a trip. But if they hop on board, they better have the ticket with them.

Why weren't we introduced?

Because sending an NTO is an important step toward securing lien rights, you would think that every lienor would send one. This is not always the case. A lienor may not send an NTO if he was paid for his service within the statutory deadline for sending one. For example, in Florida a lienor must send the NTO within 45 days of the first day on the job. Consider a small project where a lienor begins work on Day 1, completes the work on Day 10, and is paid in full on Day 15. Because the lienor was paid before the deadline for sending an NTO expired, the lienor may not send the NTO. But know this: lienors that do send a Notice to Owner as prescribed by law have taken an important step toward securing their lien rights. Therefore it is essential to ensure that they are paid.

 A general contractor may not be required by law to send you an NTO even though he may be a lienor. This is because you contracted with him directly (i.e., you are "in privity" with him) and are therefore aware of his presence. No introductions are necessary.

Owner's duties under lien law

Now that you know who your lienors are, you must perform certain duties to protect your property from liens. Your primary duty? To ensure that your lienors are paid. In Florida, if you make **proper payments** under the lien statute, you have a complete defense against claims of lien. Proper payments are those in which a **lien release** (also known as waiver of lien, release of lien, and waiver and release of lien) is exchanged for a payment. A lien release is a brief document that states that the lienor waives any right to claim a lien for the labor, services, and materials provided *through the date of the waiver*. **Therefore a lien release acts as a receipt and must be provided by all lienors in exchange for payments to them.** If you are an owner/builder and paying the lienors directly, you will obtain the lien releases. If you have hired a general contractor who is paying the lienors, he or she will obtain the lien releases at time of payment and can provide them to you. But regardless of who collects the lien releases, you should take an active role and track them because liens are bad news.

 As a general rule, if the project is financed with a construction loan, the lender will obtain lien releases before disbursing funds to the general contractor.

Behold the Lieniator

Types of lien releases

There are basically two types of lien releases used in the construction industry. They are the partial lien release and the final lien release. A ***partial lien release*** is exchanged for a partial payment (of the total contract amount). A ***final lien release*** is exchanged at final payment.

The following is an example of how proper payments could be made to a lienor.

Let's say a plumber was contracted to install the plumbing in a new house. The total contract amount was $20,000. The plumber was paid this amount in three payments, or draws, as follows:

1. $7,000 on June 1, 2009
2. $8,000 on August 1, 2009
3. $5,000 on October 1, 2009

- The first payment for $7,000 was exchanged for a partial lien release in the amount of $7,000 and dated June 1, 2009.
- The second payment for $8,000 was exchanged for a partial lien release in the amount of $8,000 and dated August 1, 2009.
- The final payment for $5,000 was exchanged for a final lien release in the amount of $5,000 and dated October 1, 2009.

Therefore, the plumber was paid $20,000 and the owner received lien releases totaling $20,000. But more importantly, liens were released up to October 1, 2009. Note that many times the final lien release amount will contain a nominal figure such as $10 and not the actual amount owed. This is because lien releases are generally tracked by date rather than by the amount of payment.

Contractors sometimes ask owners to pay a deposit for materials. In order for this payment to be "proper," it must be exchanged for a lien release.

Your safety net

Keeping track of lien releases can be challenging because not only do the lienors need to be identified, their lien releases must be obtained. Large projects, for example, may have up to 20 lienors. With these multiple lienors and their payment requests, it is easy for a lien

EXAMPLE OF A PARTIAL LIEN RELEASE

Owner: Dottie Smith
General Contractor: New Home Production, Inc.
Subcontractor: IMA Plumber, Inc.

PARTIAL WAIVER AND RELEASE OF LIEN

THE UNDERSIGNED LIENOR, IN CONSIDERATION OF THE SUM OF **$7,000**, HEREBY RELEASES ITS LIEN AND RIGHT TO CLAIM A LIEN FOR LABOR, SERVICES, OR MATERIALS FURNISHED THROUGH (DATE) **June 1, 2009** TO (CUSTOMER) **New Home Production, Inc** ON THE JOB OF (OWNER) **Dottie Smith** TO THE FOLLOWING PROPERTY: (DESCRIPTION OF PROPERTY) **2020 New Homes Way, Anytown, FL 55584**

THIS WAIVER AND RELEASE DOES NOT COVER ANY RETENTION OR LABOR, SERVICES, OR MATERIALS FURNISHED AFTER THE DATE SPECIFIED.

DATE: **June 1, 2009**
BY: (LIENOR) JOHN HANCOCK
       John Hancock — President of IMA Plumber, Inc.

STATE OF **Florida**
COUNTY OF **Orange**

SWORN TO (OR AFFIRMED) AND SUBSCRIBED BEFORE ME THIS **1st** DAY OF **June, 2009** BY **John Hancock** WHO ☐ IS PERSONALLY KNOWN TO ME OR ☒ HAS PRODUCED **DL H85783895** ☐ DID TAKE AN OATH ☒ DID NOT TAKE AN OATH.

(SIGNATURE OF NOTARY PUBLIC) *Nancy Notary*

NANCY NOTARY
COMMISSION # DO 5555555
EXPIRES: 02/17/2010

(PRINT, TYPE OR STAMP COMMISSIONED NAME OF NOTARY PUBLIC)

EXAMPLE OF A FINAL LIEN RELEASE

Owner: Dottie Smith
General Contractor: New Home Production, Inc.
Subcontractor: IMA Plumber, Inc.

FINAL WAIVER AND RELEASE OF LIEN

THE UNDERSIGNED LIENOR, IN CONSIDERATION OF THE SUM OF **$5,000**, HEREBY RELEASES ITS LIEN AND RIGHT TO CLAIM A LIEN FOR LABOR, SERVICES, OR MATERIALS FURNISHED THROUGH (DATE) **October 1, 2009** TO (CUSTOMER) **New Home Production, Inc** ON THE JOB OF (OWNER) **Dottie Smith** TO THE FOLLOWING PROPERTY: (DESCRIPTION OF PROPERTY) **2020 New Homes Way, Anytown, FL 55584**

DATE: **October 1, 2009**
BY: (LIENOR) JOHN HANCOCK
      John Hancock — President of IMA Plumber, Inc.

STATE OF **Florida**
COUNTY OF **Orange**

SWORN TO (OR AFFIRMED) AND SUBSCRIBED BEFORE ME THIS **1st** DAY OF **October, 2009** BY **John Hancock** WHO ☐ IS PERSONALLY KNOWN TO ME OR ☒ HAS PRODUCED **DL H85783895** ☐ DID TAKE AN OATH ☒ DID NOT TAKE AN OATH.

NANCY NOTARY
COMMISSION # DO 5555555
EXPIRES: 02/17/2010

(SIGNATURE OF NOTARY PUBLIC) *Nancy Notary*
(PRINT, TYPE OR STAMP COMMISSIONED NAME OF NOTARY PUBLIC)

---

release to be overlooked, thereby exposing your property to a claim of lien.

There is also the matter of latecomers to your project, such as landscape contractors. In Florida, landscape contractors, like all lienors, have 45 days (from their first day on the project) in which to send their NTO. Because landscapers often do not begin their work until the close of a project, their NTO may arrive well after the project is complete. Because you may not know of this lienor and whether he has been paid, lien laws have provisions that alert you to his presence.

(General) contractor's final payment affidavit

Although it is generally true that bad news travels fast, this is not the case with a claim of lien. For example, in Florida a claim of lien can be filed within 90 days of the lienor's last day on the job! To avoid this unwanted surprise, it is very important that you know which lienors are owed money and how much they are owed at the conclusion of your project. The *contractor's final payment affidavit* (as written in the Florida statutes) does just this and you must have your general contractor complete it *before* final payment is made. By executing this affidavit, the general contractor swears under oath that all the work under the contract has been fully completed and all lienors under the direct contract have been paid in full except those listed on the affidavit. If unpaid lienors are listed, the amounts they are owed are also stated.

Unpaid lienors

Because there are instances when a general contractor requests final payment before he or she pays the subcontractors and suppliers, you may see unpaid lienors listed on the final payment affidavit. If this is the case, you must ensure that these lienors are paid in full and obtain their final lien releases. The manner in which you accomplish this can vary and should be discussed with your general contractor or legal counsel. A couple of possibilities may be:

1. Write one joint check (containing the names of the general contractor and the unpaid lienors) for the balance due the general contractor, and obtain final lien releases from all these entities in exchange for payment.

2. Pay the lienors directly, obtain their final lien releases, and then deduct these amounts from the general contractor's final payment amount. Because the final payment amount to the general contractor would change, and the unpaid lienor would be eliminated, the final payment affidavit should be edited to show these changes.

EXAMPLE OF A CONTRACTOR'S
FINAL PAYMENT AFFIDAVIT

Owner: Dottie Smith
General Contractor: New Home Production, Inc.

CONTRACTORS FINAL PAYMENT AFFIDAVIT

STATE OF **Florida**
COUNTY OF **Orange**

BEFORE ME, THE UNDERSIGNED AUTHORITY, PERSONALLY APPEARED (NAME OF AFFIANT) **Tom Builder**, WHO, AFTER BEING FIRST DULY SWORN, DEPOSES AND SAYS OF HIS OR HER PERSONAL KNOWLEDGE THE FOLLOWING:

1. **He/**SHE IS THE (TITLE) **President** OF (COMPANY) **New Home Production, Inc**, WHICH DOES BUSINESS IN THE STATE OF FLORIDA, HEREINAFTER REFERRED TO AS "CONTRACTOR"

2. CONTRACTOR, PURSUANT TO A CONTRACT WITH (OWNER) **Dottie Smith**, HEREINAFTER REFERRED TO AS THE "OWNER," HAS FURNISHED OR CAUSED TO BE FURNISHED LABOR, MATERIALS, AND SERVICES FOR THE CONSTRUCTION OF CERTAIN IMPROVEMENTS TO REAL PROPERTY DESCRIBED AS: (LEGAL DESCRIPTION)
   WEST LAKE ESTATE UNIT 2 PB 2 PG 108 LOT 29 09-26-30
   (Street address) 2020 New Home Way, Anytown, FL 55584

3. THIS AFFIDAVIT IS MADE PURSUANT TO SECTION 713.06 FLORIDA STATUTES, FOR THE PURPOSE OF INDUCING FULL PAYMENT FROM THE OWNER IN THE AMOUNT OF **$15,000**.

4. ALL WORK TO BE PERFORMED UNDER THE CONTRACT HAS BEEN FULLY COMPLETED, AND ALL LIENORS UNDER THE DIRECT CONTRACT HAVE BEEN PAID IN FULL, EXCEPT THE FOLLOWING LISTED LIENORS:

   NAME OF LIENOR **N/A**   AMOUNT DUE _____

SIGNED, SEALED AND DELIVERED THIS **29th** DAY OF **November, 2009**
BY: (AFFIANT) TOM BUILDER
   Tom Builder — President of New Home Production, Inc.

SWORN TO (OR AFFIRMED) AND SUBSCRIBED BEFORE ME THIS **29th** DAY OF **November, 2009** BY **Tom Builder** WHO ☐ IS PERSONALLY KNOWN TO ME OR ☒ HAS PRODUCED **DL B89385762** ☒ DID TAKE AN OATH ☐ DID NOT TAKE AN OATH.

(SIGNATURE OF NOTARY PUBLIC) *Nancy Notary*
MY COMMISSION EXPIRES: **02/17/2010**

NANCY NOTARY
COMMISSION # DO 5555555
EXPIRES. 02/17/2010

You should also know that there may be provisions in your state's lien laws that require the contractor to provide you with information such as a statement of accounts as well as contracts with lienors. In the Florida statutes, these provisions fall under "Section 713.16: Demand for copy of contract and statement of account."

As an extra precaution against liens, you can ask your subcontractors to sign a sworn document which states that all of their suppliers and/or sub-subcontractors have been paid in full. Absent a prohibition in your state's lien laws, such language could be incorporated into the subcontractor's final lien release.

Know thy lien laws

It is generally acknowledged that all rights have a corresponding duty. In order to realize all the protections afforded by lien law, generally you and the lienor must strictly comply with its highly detailed rules and procedures. The following is a brief overview of some of the rules and procedures in Florida.

A few Florida lien facts (as of 2009)

- Lienor must send a Notice to Owner within 45 days of the first day on the job.
- The claim of lien must be recorded within 90 days of the last day on the job.
- The claim of lien must be recorded in the county where the property is located.
- The claim of lien must be served to the owner within 15 days of recording.
- The claim of lien is effective for one year unless the owner records a "notice of contest of lien" or files a "lawsuit to show cause."
- A "lawsuit to foreclose a construction lien" must be filed before one year or the lien becomes null and void.
- The lienor must hold a state (professional) license, if his trade is licensed by the state.
- Claims of lien can only be claimed for work that is permanent in nature. (Landscaping maintenance and pool maintenance are not eligible.)
- Small contracts are exempt from lien action if the prime contract is less than $2,500. (Note that there are exemptions to this rule.)

LIEN PREVENTION CHECKLIST

☐ 1. Understand your state's lien laws including who has lien rights and the lienor's deadlines for filing NTO and related documents.

☐ 2. Create a list of all lienors from the list given you from the general contractor and from the NTOs that you receive.

☐ 3. Obtain lien waivers from all lienors in exchange for payment.

☐ 4. Obtain a final payment affidavit from general contractor.

☐ 5. Obtain proof of payment from all lienors (as additional protection).

☐ 6. Require all lienors to notarize their lien waivers and affidavits.

☐ 7. Require the general contractor to incorporate language into his contracts with subcontractors that forbids them from hiring other subcontractors.

The Lieniator says ...

The right to claim lien has been enacted in a majority of states and each one has unique and complicated lien laws. Strict compliance with these requirements is generally necessary for a claim of lien to be legally binding. A contractor who does not abide by these rigid requirements may lose monies owned him. On the other hand, if you do not make proper payments under a lien statute, you may pay twice for work performed as the result of a claim of lien. If this debt goes unpaid, your house may be sold in a foreclosure sale with the monies going toward the amounts claimed by lien.

Because lien law is very complex and unique to each state, and because liens can be financially devastating, many state statutes recommend that you consult a construction attorney who is knowledgeable about state lien law. These attorneys practice "preventative counseling" in an effort to prevent costly problems before they occur. Therefore if you do not understand lien law, or if you do not have the time to properly manage lien-related documents, it is prudent to seek counsel with a knowledgeable attorney who specializes in construction law at the outset of your project. This professional can provide legal advice specific to your project.

Don't forget that a payment bond is your alternative to the complicated and tiresome matter of policing Notice to Owners, lien releases, and contractor affidavits. Read more about payment bonds in Chapter 7.

EXAMPLE OF A CLAIM OF LIEN

Owner: Fred Smith
General Contractor: Mayday Construction, Inc.
Subcontractor (Lienor): Build Right Carpenters, Inc.

WARNING! THIS LEGAL DOCUMENT REFLECTS THAT A CONSTRUCTION LIEN HAS BEEN PLACED ON THE REAL PROPERTY LISTED HEREIN. UNLESS THE OWNER OF SUCH PROPERTY TAKES ACTION TO SHORTEN THE TIME PERIOD, THIS LIEN SHALL REMAIN VALID FOR ONE YEAR FROM THE DATE OF RECORDING, AND SHALL EXPIRE AND BECOME NULL AND VOID THEREAFTER UNLESS LEGAL PROCEEDINGS HAVE BEEN COMMENCED TO FORECLOSE OR DISCHARGE THIS LIEN.

CLAIM OF LIEN

STATE OF *Florida*
COUNTY OF *Orange*

BEFORE ME, THE UNDERSIGNED NOTARY PUBLIC, PERSONALLY APPEARED *Carl Carpenter,* WHO WAS DULY SWORN AND SAYS THAT *he*/SHE IS THE *President* OF THE LIENOR HEREIN, *Build Right Carpenters Inc.* WHOSE ADDRESS IS *2454 Payme Avenue, Anytown, FL 55584* AND THAT IN ACCORDANCE WITH A CONTRACT WITH *Mayday Construction, Inc.*, LIENOR FURNISHED LABOR, SERVICES, OR MATERIALS CONSISTING OF *labor and materials to build a 10'x20' wood porch* ON THE FOLLOWING DESCRIBED REAL PROPERTY IN *Orange County, Florida.*
LEGAL DESCRIPTION OF REAL PROPERTY: *PINE TREE ESTATE UNIT 2 PB 2 PG 92 95 LOT 21 09-26-30. Street Address — 123 Ridge Rd. Anytown, FL 55582*

OWNED BY: *Fred Smith* OF A TOTAL VALUE OF *$10,250*, OF WHICH THERE REMAINS UNPAID *$4,100*, AND FURNISHED THE FIRST OF THE ITEMS ON *April 14, 2009* AND THE LAST OF THE ITEMS ON *April 24, 2009* AND IF THE LIEN IS CLAIMED BY ONE NOT IN PRIVITY WITH THE OWNER, THAT THE LIENOR SERVED HIS NOTICE TO OWNER ON *April 20, 2009* BY *U.S. certified mail, return receipt number R890047878278* AND IF REQUIRED, THAT THE LIENOR SERVED COPIES OF THE NOTICE ON THE CONTRACTOR ON *N/A* BY _____, AND ON THE SUBCONTRACTOR *N/A* BY _____

DATE: *October 1, 2009*
BY: (LIENOR) *CARL CARPENTER*
            Carl Carpenter — President of Build Right Carpenters, Inc.

SWORN TO (OR AFFIRMED) AND SUBSCRIBED BEFORE ME THIS *1st* DAY OF *October, 2009* BY *Carl Carpenter — President of Build Right Carpenters Inc.*
WHO ☐ IS PERSONALLY KNOWN TO ME OR ☒ HAS PRODUCED *DL C625773857656* ☒ DID TAKE AN OATH ☐ DID NOT TAKE AN OATH.

(SIGNATURE OF NOTARY PUBLIC) *Nancy Notary*
MY COMMISION EXPIRES: *02/17/2010*

NANCY NOTARY
COMMISSION # DO 5555555
EXPIRES: 02/17/2010

EXAMPLE OF A FLORIDA LIEN SEQUENCE

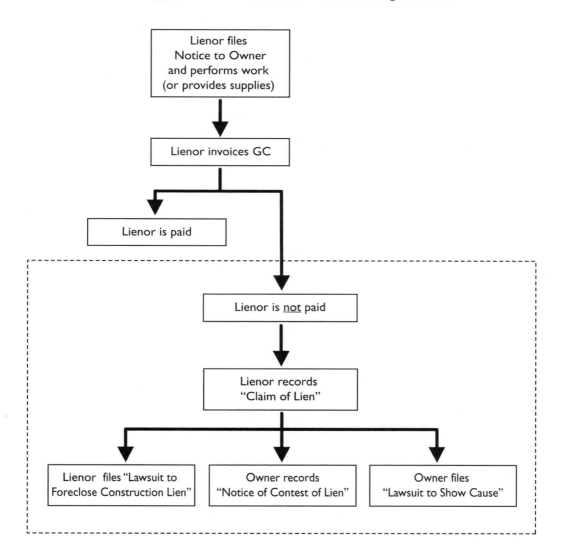

14

OTHER PROJECT CONSIDERATIONS

Disclaimer: The following information is presented as a general overview of some of the hazards that may be present on a jobsite. To learn more about potential hazards and their remedies, read the Occupational Safety and Health Administration's (OSHA) guidelines at www.osha.gov.

Often authority and responsibility are mistakenly assumed to go hand in hand. For example, a contractor may have the authority to do your work, but he or she may not assume the responsibility for the outcome.

Construction can be a costly undertaking even when things go as planned. When jobsite injuries and disputes occur, construction slows and becomes more costly. Jobsite safety and record keeping are important tasks that protect you from the loss of time and money. Even though contractors routinely perform these tasks, you should do the same because your participation helps to ensure the success of your project.

Avoiding the calm in complacency

Because construction has a high occurrence of injury and death, it is considered a hazardous occupation. Therefore workers' compensation insurance must be in place as a means of protection. Unfortunately, this insurance does not protect against the loss of morale and productivity that occurs when an injury happens. Nor does insurance prevent the physical suffering that results from an injury. Although insurance is an asset after an injury has occurred, injuries are best avoided altogether. Here is some help with this matter.

Safety sleuths

The Occupational Safety and Health Administration (OSHA) issues and enforces workplace safety and health rules (called standards) that protect America's working men and women. Since 1971 when the Occupational Safety and Health Act was passed, these standards have helped to reduce workplace fatalities by more than 60% and occupation illness and injury by 40%. The goal of the Occupational Safety and Health Act—and the Occupational Safety and Health Administration—is to ensure that employers provide employees with a safe work environment.

One of the roles that OSHA performs is to collect data about workplace injuries, illness, and death. This data reveals that most construction-related injuries and death result from:

- Falls from elevations such as roofs, platforms, stairs, and ladders
- Impact from falling objects and vehicles
- Being caught in cave-ins, and unguarded machinery or equipment
- Electrical shock

To help prevent jobsite injuries, illness, and death, OSHA developed rules that require employers to train their employees and communicate information to them. Training often addresses:

- Proper use of jobsite equipment and machines
- Handling of harmful substances such as flammable, caustic, and poisonous chemicals
- Use of personal protective equipment such as gloves, protective eyewear, and respirators
- Availability of medical care and fire protection on the jobsite
- General protective measures as they apply to the trade being performed

OSHA recognizes employees' "right to know" about the hazards they are exposed to in the workplace, thereby allowing employees to take precautions against harmful effects of workplace hazards. With an awareness of jobsite hazards and the implementation of safety measures, jobsite injury and illness have been reduced.

Fall injuries

Falls are one of the leading causes of injury and death in the construction industry and they often occur from roofs, scaffolds, and ladders. To prevent injury from falling, OSHA generally requires fall protection such as guardrails, safety nets, and personal fall arrestors in areas higher than 6 feet. Barriers should also be placed around unprotected floor and roof openings at skylights, stairwells, shafts, etc. Because open trenches can also present a fall hazard, they should be well marked.

Scaffolds are used frequently during construction; when improperly erected, they can lead to accidents. For example, scaffolds can collapse, causing severe injury and damage. Also, improperly installed guardrails and planking can give way, causing a worker to fall. Therefore a trained person should oversee erection of the scaffold and continually inspect it for stability and damaged parts.

Stairways and ladders also contribute to many falls. Because of this, guardrails should be installed in stairways with more than a 30-inch rise and the stairway landings must be of sufficient size. Falls from ladders can result from a ladder being positioned on unstable ground. Even when properly placed, the workers must evenly distribute their weight to prevent the ladder from overturning.

Poorly located debris, materials, and equipment can also cause a person to trip. Therefore air hoses, electrical cords, and ropes should be coiled up and placed aside when not in use. Stored materials should also be well-organized and placed outside the immediate work area. When the jobsite is kept clean and organized, injury from trips or falls is less likely to occur.

FALLS BY TYPE

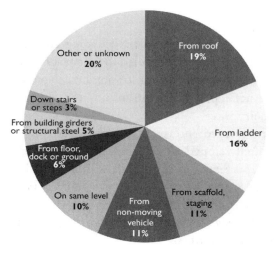

Of the 847 fatal falls in 2007, over one-third involved falls from roofs or ladders.

NOTE: Percentages may not add to totals because of rounding.

Source: U.S. Bureau of Labor Statistics, U.S. Department of Labor, 2009

Excavation

Excavation takes place on many construction projects because the building pad must be prepared, pipes need to be buried, and the ground, in general, must be contoured. Excavation is particularly dangerous because both the act of digging and the resulting excavated areas can be unsafe. While excavation is underway, electrocution and explosion can occur if underground services, such as electric and gas lines, are broken. This hazardous situation can be avoided by working closely with utility locators who can identify and mark existing underground utilities.

Because damaged utilities can be disruptive and dangerous, the government created a *Dig Safely* program. This program includes a service called *One Call*. All it takes is one phone call from you, and all utility providers who are affected by your excavation are notified. They, in turn, locate and mark the utilities on your property with colored flags that are coded as follows:

American Public Works Association (APWA) color code of underground utilities

Red = electric

Orange = communication

Blue = water

Green = sewer

Purple = reclaimed water

Pink = temporary survey marking

White = proposed excavation

When contacting One Call, be prepared to report your contact information, jobsite address, and the depth of digging that is scheduled to take place. When possible, use white paint to mark the area to be excavated on your jobsite. Once your request is submitted, it can be tracked on the Internet. This allows you to monitor which locators will visit your jobsite and the status of their visit.

Once excavation is performed, preventative measures must be taken to prevent collapse. By creating gradually sloped trench banks, cave-ins can be prevented. When sloped banks are not viable, protective systems such as shoring and shielding must be used to stabilize the soil. If workers need to enter an excavated area, they must have sufficient air and light, as well as a means of exit. The excavated area should also be well marked so that the workers do not fall. *Because excavated areas can be hazardous, they should be backfilled as soon as the work is complete.*

Cranes and other hoisting equipment

Cranes and other hoisting equipment are often used to lift construction materials. When

While hoisting and excavation is under way, workers should monitor overhead electric lines as well as equipment, structures, and each other.

the ropes, slings, and chains used to lift these materials are stressed beyond capacity, they can break. In addition, if the load is improperly balanced, the hoisting equipment may overturn. ***Therefore, never allow workers underneath a load that is being lifted and always employ competent riggers and equipment operators.*** Prior to operating the equipment, these trained workers must inspect the hoisting equipment and all rigging for damage. Riggers and equipment operators must have the capability to calculate both the load weight and the equipment's capacity to lift the load. The work area must also be closely inspected so that the equipment maintains proper clearance from potential hazards. When hoisting a load, maintain a minimum of 10 feet of clearance from overhead electrical wires. The operator must also be observant of surrounding workers, equipment, and structures.

Electrical hazards

Although sometimes overlooked as a serious hazard, electricity can cause burns, fires, and explosions. Therefore all contractors should be familiar with the project's electrical systems—especially when they are energized.

Lock out/tag out is a safety procedure used to ensure that an energized system is not turned on while someone is working on it. For example, an electrician can be seriously harmed if the electricity is turned on while he or she is working on the circuit. To prevent this from occurring, a lock-out device must be placed at the main power source, such as at the panel. When work is complete, the lock-out device should be removed by the electrical contractors who placed it there. ***No one else should remove a lock-out device!*** When the electrical system is to be reenergized, the electrician must notify all other workers before powering up. Pneumatic, hydraulic, and other pressurized systems must also be locked and tagged as a safety measure.

Vehicle safety

Site work often requires the use of heavy equipment such as bulldozers and backhoes. Because this equipment is large, the operator may have an obstructed view that prevents him from seeing a person adjacent to his machinery. This has led to many jobsite injuries; some so severe that death has resulted.

It is extremely dangerous to be behind heavy equipment, as well as directly in front of the lifting mechanism such as a loader bucket. Any worker adjacent to heavy equipment should wear a brightly colored vest to be more visible. Additionally, a co-worker should oversee the work area when heavy equipment is in operation and signal when unsafe conditions arise. Once work is complete, the equipment operator should lower and secure all lifting devices, put the gears in neutral, set the brake, and remove the key.

Fatal Facts

Jobsite injury occurs from a variety of hazards and sometimes these injuries are fatal. To help promote awareness and thereby reduce jobsite injury, OSHA has compiled a list of construction-related accident reports, *Fatal Facts*, which is available on the OSHA website at www.osha.gov/OshDoc/toc_FatalFacts.html. *Fatal Facts* lists accidents that have occurred on construction jobsites, as well as prevention recommendations. By enforcing OSHA's recommendations, jobsite injuries can be reduced.

OSHA also provides free and confidential advice in order to facilitate jobsite safety. Consultations are available to small- and medium-sized businesses, including construction companies. This service is separate from enforcement and consequently does not result in penalties or citations if violations are determined. Their only obligation is to correct any serious job safety and health hazards.

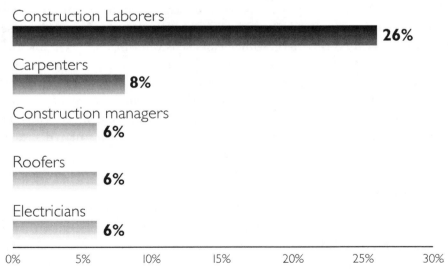

DISTRIBUTION OF FATALITIES BY SELECTED CONSTRUCTION OCCUPATIONS, 2007

Source: U.S. Bureau of Labor Statistics, U.S. Department of Labor, 2009

Other matters that matter

Just as jobsite injuries are unwanted events that are disruptive and harmful, disputes should also be avoided. Good recordkeeping is a means to prevent disputes and it will also provide you with a keepsake of your construction experience.

Agree to disagree

Disagreements are a fact of life because people are complex beings with intellect and emotions that influence their perception. Resolving these differences can be time consuming, but worse yet, disputes can cause animosity if they are handled the wrong way. For example, if a person, instead of the problem, is attacked, cooperation may break down. This irrational behavior is unproductive and can jeopardize the success of the project. Although the goal is to avoid disputes altogether, when disputes do occur, they should be promptly addressed in a professional manner.

Daily log

Construction can be a complex undertaking involving many contractors performing multiple tasks. Although information regarding these tasks is primarily conveyed through building plans and other construction documents, often information is exchanged verbally. Although this verbal exchange may appear to be acceptable at the time, many people later regret not documenting their decisions in writing. Agreements that are not recorded in some manner may be forgotten or remembered incorrectly. This can lead to misunderstandings and confrontations that negatively affect the project and the people involved with it. To avoid these misunderstandings, **a daily log should be maintained**. The daily log is a written account of matters related to your project. The logbook, which may be a simple blank journal, a preprinted ledger, or a computerized software program, should contain daily entries that address the following topics:

Work

The work section of the entry should document the work that occurred on the jobsite, how long it took, and who did it. An example of a daily log entry could read: "June 8, 2009. 8 a.m.–4:30 p.m. CC Roofing crew of 3 men nailed shingles on the roof." The entry may also contain other pertinent information such as: "The job is scheduled to be complete by June 9, 2009."

Communications

It is important to summarize communications in the daily log so that discussions and any decisions are recorded. Communications with architects, contractors, and engineers are especially important because significant issues are often addressed. Structural changes and design changes must be noted even when a written change order is executed. Payment and schedule issues should also be recorded. Although most log entries originate from meetings and jobsite discussions, the daily log should also contain information that originates from e-mail and other written communication.

Significant events

Significant events is a broad topic, which can range from the discovery of an unknown condition to unintentional damage to the property. An example of a log entry might read: "August 20, 2009. 1:30 p.m. Colby Landscaping broke pressurized main water line to house with backhoe. CC took prompt action to shut off water, repair pipe, and backfill trench. Time spent: 1 hour."

Jobsite injuries

Because jobsite injuries can have serious consequences, these injuries and the facts that surround them must be documented in the log. These entries should be highly detailed, especially if the injury is severe. This entry should include the description of the accident, the resulting injury, possible reasons for the accident, and site conditions that may have contributed to the accident. An example of a documented accident might read: "May 20, 2009, 10:30 a.m. Bob Smith of Thomas Framing Inc. fell off ladder while nailing truss strap in place resulting in an injured ankle. Bob treated ankle with ice for one hour and then left jobsite. Bob said he lost his balance even though ladder was securely positioned on firm soil at time of accident." If drug or alcohol use, horseplay, or foul play is suspected, make a note in the log and contact the general contractor.

Materials

The daily log should contain information about materials and supplies delivered to the jobsite. All delivery receipts should be reviewed to determine if the entire order was delivered. If items are missing, these back-ordered items, as well as their anticipated delivery date, should be noted in the daily log. Also, any noticeable defects should be noted. A log entry might read: "May 15, 2009, 8:00 a.m. Mid State truss package delivered. The truss package is complete without noticeable defects."

Weather

Because weather can impact a job schedule, it is important to briefly describe the weather conditions each day. It is especially important to note significant weather events, such as heavy rain, snow, or wind, that cause work to slow or stop.

Photographic Documentation

Whereas a daily log allows the author to maintain a highly detailed written account of events, photo documentation is equally important because it provides evidence of a condition or event. Whereas a close-up photo of the work may document a specific item, a wide-angle photo may reveal things such as weather, manpower, equipment, and materials on the jobsite. Because jobsite photos are used as documentation, they should have the date imprinted on them digitally, if possible.

There are additional benefits to documenting the project through photographs. Photos allow you to quickly and effectively communicate with contractors, architects, engineers, and Building Department officials if questions arise. For example, some matters can be quickly addressed via e-mail. With the addition of photos, a situation is more comprehensible and thus more readily resolved.

Photos are also useful after construction is completed. Photos of the framed walls, including all pipes and wires, allow you to see behind the wall after the drywall is hung. This information can help you determine where heavy items such as shelves can be hung. In addition, if you decide to remodel in the future, these photos will provide useful information that will help you design the project.

15
IN A NUTSHELL

Like it or not, you may have to undertake a construction project during your life. Whether it is a small household improvement such as replacing your roof shingles, or a more substantial project such as a remodel, addition, or the construction of a new home, construction is a part of many people's lives. This can be an exciting and satisfying experience—if the job is done correctly, on time and on budget—or it can be stressful and disappointing. For some, it can lead to financial ruin.

To help ensure the success of your project, it is important to understand construction contracting. Yet considering the effort involved, it may feel unsatisfying when compared to construction itself. Construction is an exciting process, especially when certain milestones are reached. When the walls and roof are complete, your project has shape. When paint and flooring come in, your dream is close to a reality. This excitement is surprisingly lacking after a long day researching your state's lien statutes and requirements for contractor licensing. Your eyes are tired, your back hurts, and all you gained is knowledge—not something you can see and touch. But know this: Your knowledge is a true foundation of your construction project. Without it, your project could fail.

Start off on the right foot

Finding a qualified contractor to perform your (clearly defined) work is an important first step. Professional licensing, when required by your state, is essential because licensing demonstrates that a person has met state standards for his or her profession. Because these standards generally address both trade knowledge and experience, a licensed contractor is more likely to provide the professional service you deserve.

Contractor insurance is also important because it protects you when things go wrong. Jobsite injury can occur because construction is dangerous. Contractors use powerful equipment such as nail guns and saws—sometimes while balancing precariously on ladders and roofs. Heavy equipment, such as front end loaders, can also injure a worker who may not be attentive. Because jobsite injury can be severe and long lasting, it is essential that insurance is in place to protect you from loss.

But keep this in mind: Although your state has safeguards in place to protect you and the public, the burden falls on you to verify that a contractor meets these state requirements. This information is readily available on state websites and at your local Building Department. In addition, you are well served to do further research. From government records to personal blogs, there is an abundance of information that can be analyzed to judge a contractor's character and performance. Through your investigative efforts, you are likely to find a qualified contractor with integrity and experience.

Integrity starts with "I"

In order for a project to be truly successful, integrity is required by both you and the contractor. If you demand professional service, you should be willing to pay a fair price for it. Heed the words of conmen who claim that "you can't cheat an honest man." This is because a conman's success often depends on your ability to be misled. If greed clouds your judgment, you may make a foolish decision. Consider these words if a contractor proposes an unreasonably low price for your work. If it sounds too good to be true, it probably is, and you may pay for it in the long run.

Once you receive a proposal from a tried-and-true contractor, a clearly written and inclusive contract is necessary. A good contract, like a good fence, makes for a good relationship because it clearly defines parameters. Misunderstandings are less likely to occur with a good contract and well-defined scope of work. To further reduce misunderstandings, document all verbal agreements relevant to your project as well as the work itself. Through well-written plans, contracts, and observations, misunderstanding are less likely to turn into nonproductive "he said, she said" disputes.

Risk versus benefits

Common sense plays a big role in the success of a building project. CONtractors often encourage homeowners to pull the permit for them or avoid the matter entirely. Permitting is in place to protect you, your family, and the public. Building inspections, which are conducted following the issuance of a permit, ensure that the work is code compliant. If your work is not to code, you do not benefit from the knowledge of learned professionals who thoroughly study building methods and materials to ensure their soundness.

Also consider this: When you build without a permit, it is often not a question of if you will get caught, but rather, when you will get caught. Your local government has code compliancy officers that look for non-permitted construction work. Sometimes a ladder, portable toilet, or dumpster alerts them while other times an angry neighbor reports you. In addition, the Property Appraiser's Office continually checks homes in its jurisdiction to ensure that its information is current and correct. If a home shows increased square footage (such as an addition) or additional improvements (such as a pool), this information may be forwarded to the Building Department. Realtors, lenders, and appraisers may also contact the Building Department regarding improvements that show up on surveys that are performed when a house is to be sold.

Once the Building Department is aware of unpermitted work on your property, you may be fined. To make matters worse, you may have to get your project permitted after all. This can be costly because the permitting process becomes more difficult. For example, if building plans are required, the architect may need you to expose work that is hidden from view. Pipes, wires, and fasteners must also be viewed by the building inspector. Therefore you may have to demolish (some of) your completed work, have it inspected, and then rebuild it again. Not only will the existing work be damaged, a trusting relationship with the inspector may be damaged as well. With this much at stake, ask yourself if the benefit of forgoing permitting is worth the risk.

To be or not to be

Assuming the risk and responsibility of a contractor should also be considered before you take on the role of owner/builder. As owner/builder, you are responsible for supervision, performance, safety, taxes, and other matters. If you hire unlicensed contractors, you may be considered an employer and subsequently be obligated to pay payroll taxes, unemployment taxes, and workers' compensation. If you fail to do so, the penalties may be severe. Although many people have successfully performed as owner/builder, others have fallen short because they lack the skill and time to be effective. If you feel you are unprepared to fill the role of owner/builder, consider hiring a qualified contractor and learn from the experience. Reputable contractors are often willing to share their knowledge with those who show an interest in construction. Once you learn the ropes, you should be better prepared to act as owner/builder when your next project comes along.

Regardless of which route you choose, you should always participate in a meaningful way and work together with all contractors toward the shared goal of success. Remember that frequent and clear communication is essential. Ask questions as needed and provide input regarding any matters that require clarification. You should also let the contractors know if they are performing as agreed. If the contracting parties are clear about their duties and perform them correctly in a professional and timely manner, you will likely find that both the journey and the outcome are rewarding.

APPENDIX

Appendix A - Noteworthy Organizations

Organization	Website	Phone Number
CONSTRUCTION		
American Institute of Architects	www.aia.org	202-242-3837
National Association of Home Builders	www.nahb.org	202-266-8200
Associated General Contractors of America	www.agc.org	703-548-3118
Associated Builders and Contractors	www.abc.org	703-812-2000
American Subcontractors Association	www.asaonline.com	703-684-3450
National Fire Protection Association	www.dfpa.org	617-770-3000
American Public Works Association	www.apwa.net	202-408-9541
Dig Safely	www.call811.com	811
U.S. Green Building Council	www.usgbc.org	800-795-1747
Energy Star	www.energystar.gov	800-782-7937
LICENSING		
National Association of State Contractor's Licensing	www.nascla.org	623-587-9354
Energy Star	www.energystar.gov	800-782-7937
WORKERS' COMPENSATION		
U.S. Department of Labor	www.dol.gov	800-333-4636
National Council on Compensation Insurance	www.ncii.com	561-893-1000
INSURANCE		
Insurance Information Institute	www.iii.org	212-346-5500
National Association of Insurance Commissioners	www.naic.org	816-842-3600
BUILDING CODES		
International Code Council	www.iccsafe.org	888-422-7233
LAND USE CODES/LOCAL ORDINANCES		
Municipal Code Council	www.municode.com	850-576-3171
SAFETY		
Occupational Safety and Health Administration	www.osha.gov	800-333-4636
LAW		
American Bar Association	www.abanet.org	312-988-5000

CONSUMER PROTECTION		
Federal Trade Commission	www.ftc.gov	800-333-4636
Consumer Action	www.consumeraction.gov	800-333-4636
Better Business Bureau	www.bbb.org	
Angie's List	www.angieslist.com	
Consumer Reports	www.consumerreports.org	866-208-9427
BONDS		
Surety Information Office	www.sio.org	202-686-7463
Surety and Fidelity Association of America	www.surety,org	202-686-7463
FEDERAL GOVERNMENT		
Government Made Easy	www.usa.gov	800-333-4636
EMERGENCY MANAGEMENT		
FEMA	www.fema.gov	800-333-4636
HOME OWNERSHIP		
U.S. Census Bureau	www.census.gov	800-333-4636
U.S. Housing and Urban Development	www.hud.gov	800-333-4636
URBAN PLANNING		
American Planning Association	www.planning.org	202-872-0611
COURTS		
National Association for State Courts	www.ncsonline.org	703-841-0200
TAXES		
Internal Revenue Service	www.irs.gov	800-829-1040

Appendix B — U.S. State Governments

State	Website
Alabama	www.alabama.gov
Alaska	www.state.ak.us
Arizona	www.az.gov
Arkansas	www.state.ar.us
California	www.ca.gov
Colorado	www.colorado.gov
Connecticut	www.ct.gov
Delaware	www.delaware.gov

State	Website
District of Columbia	www.dc.gov
Florida	www.myflorida.com
Georgia	www.georgia.gov
Hawaii	www.ehawaii.gov
Idaho	www.idaho.gov
Illinois	www.illinois.gov
Indiana	www.in.gov
Iowa	www.iowa.gov
Kansas	www.kansas.gov
Kentucky	www.kentucky.gov
Louisiana	www.louisiana.gov
Maine	www.maine.gov
Maryland	www.maryland.gov
Massachusetts	www.state.ma.us
Michigan	www.michigan.gov
Minnesota	www.state.mn.us
Mississippi	www.mississippi.gov
Missouri	www.missouri.gov
Montana	www.mt.gov
Nebraska	www.nebraska.gov
Nevada	www.nv.gov
New Hampshire	www.nh.gov
New Jersey	www.nj.gov
New Mexico	www.newmexico.gov
New York	www.state.ny.us
N. Carolina	www.ncgov.com
N. Dakota	www.nd.gov
Ohio	www.ohio.gov
Oklahoma	www.ok.gov
Oregon	www.oregon.gov
Pennsylvania	www.state.pa.us
Rhode Island	www.ri.gov
S. Carolina	www.sc.gov
S. Dakota	www.state.sd.us
Tennessee	www.state.tn.us
Texas	www.texas.gov
Utah	www.utah.gov
Vermont	www.vermont.gov
Virginia	www.virginia.gov
Washington	www.access.wa.gov
W. Virginia	www.wv.gov
Wisconsin	www.wisconsin.gov
Wyoming	www.wyoming.gov

Appendix C - State Professional Licensing Divisions

State	State Website	Contractor Licensing Website	Phone Number
Alabama	www.alabama.gov	www.genconbd.alabama.gov	(334) 272-5030
Alaska	www.state.ak.us	http://www.labor.state.ak.us/research/dlo/contrcon.htm	(907) 465-8443
Arizona	www.az.gov	www.rc.state.az.us	(602) 542-1525
Arkansas	www.state.ar.us	www.state.ar.us/clb	(501) 372-4661
California	www.ca.gov	www.cslb.ca.gov	(800) 321-2752
Colorado	www.colorado.gov	www.dora.state.co.us	(303) 894-7855
Connecticut	www.ct.gov	www.ct.gov/dcp	(800) 842-2649
Delaware	www.delaware.gov	https://dorweb.revenue.delaware.gov/bussrch/	(302)744 4500
D.C.	www.dc.gov	http://brc.dc.gov/licenses/licenses.asp	(202) 442-4400
Florida	www.myflorida.com	www.myflorida.com/dbpr	(850) 487-1395
Georgia	www.georgia.gov	www.sos.georgia.gov	(404) 656-2817
Hawaii	www.ehawaii.gov	http://hawaii.gov/dcca/areas/pvl/boards/contractor/	(808) 586-2700
Idaho	www.idaho.gov	https://secure.ibol.idaho.gov/IBOL/Home.aspx	(208) 334-3233
Illinois	www.illinois.gov	www.idfpr.com	(217) 785-0800
Indiana	www.in.gov	http://www.in.gov/pla/	(800) 457-8283
Iowa	www.iowa.gov	http://www.iowalifechanging.com/business/blic.aspx	(515) 242-4755
Kansas	www.kansas.gov	http://www.da.ks.gov/fp/contractor/default.htm	(785) 296-2113
Kentucky	www.kentucky.gov	http://www.bgky.org/contractorslicensing/index.php	(270) 781-3530
Louisiana	www.louisiana.gov	www.lslbc.louisiana.gov	(225) 765-2301
Maine	www.maine.gov	www.maine.gov/pfr	(207) 624-8500
Maryland	www.maryland.gov	http://blis.state.md.us/LicenseDetail.aspx?LicenseIDs=302	(410) 230-6169
Massachusetts	www.state.ma.us	http://www.mass.gov/?pageID=mg2constituent&L=2&L0=Home&L1=Business&sid=massgov2	(866) 888-2808
Michigan	www.michigan.gov	http://www.michigan.gov/som/0,1607,7-192-29943_31469---,00.html	(877) 766-1779
Minnesota	www.state.mn.us	http://www.state.mn.us/license/content.do?mode=license&LicenseID=5534	(651) 284-5065
Mississippi	www.mississippi.gov	http://www.msboc.us/	(601)354-6161
Missouri	www.missouri.gov	http://www.pr.mo.gov/	(573) 751-0293
Montana	www.mt.gov	http://mtcontractor.com/crx/CRWelcome.htm	(406) 444 2840
Nebraska	www.nebraska.gov	http://www.dhhs.ne.gov/licensing.htm	(402) 471-3121
Nevada	www.nv.gov	http://www.nvcontractorsboard.com/	(775) 688-1141
New Hampshire	www.nh.gov	http://www.nh.gov/nhes/elmi/licertreg.htm	(603)228-4124
New Jersey	www.nj.gov	http://www.nj.gov/njbusiness/licenses/	(866) 534-7789
New Mexico	www.newmexico.gov	http://www.rld.state.nm.us/CID/index.htm	(505) 476-4700
New York	www.state.ny.us	http://www.gorr.state.ny.us/	(518) 474-8275
N. Carolina	www.ncgov.com	http://www.nccommerce.com/en/BusinessServices/StartYourBusiness/BusinessLicensesPermits/	(919) 733-4151
N. Dakota	www.nd.gov	http://www.nd.gov/sos/licensing/	(701) 328-3665
Ohio	www.ohio.gov	http://www.com.state.oh.us/dic/dicocilb.htm	(614) 644-3493
Oklahoma	www.ok.gov	http://www.ok.gov/cib/	(405) 271-5217
Oregon	www.oregon.gov	http://www.oregon.gov/CCB/index.shtml	(503) 378-4621

State	State Website	Contractor Licensing Website	Phone Number
Pennsylvania	www.state.pa.us	http://www.dos.state.pa.us/dos/site/default.asp	(717) 787 8503
Rhode Island	www.ri.gov	http://www.crb.ri.gov	(401) 222-1268
S. Carolina	www.sc.gov	http://www.llr.state.sc.us/POL/Contractors/	(803) 896-4501
S. Dakota	www.state.sd.us	http://www.state.sd.us/dol/lmic/careerrelatedsiteslicensing.htm	(605)773-3311
Tennessee	www.state.tn.us	http://tennessee.gov/commerce/boards/contractors/	(615) 741-8307
Texas	www.texas.gov	http://www.license.state.tx.us	(512) 463-6599
Utah	www.utah.gov	http://www.dopl.utah.gov/	(801) 530-6628
Vermont	www.vermont.gov	http://www.vermont.gov/portal/business/index.php?id=93	(802)479 7561
Virginia	www.virginia.gov	http://www.dba.virginia.gov/vbic.shtml	(804) 371-0438
Washington	www.access.wa.gov	http://www.lni.wa.gov/TradesLicensing/Contractors/default.asp	(800) 647-0982
W. Virginia	www.wv.gov	http://www.wv.gov/licensing/Pages/default.aspx	(304) 558-7890
Wisconsin	www.wisconsin.gov	http://www.wisconsin.gov/state/core/business.html	(608) 266 2112
Wyoming	www.wyoming.gov	http://governor.wy.gov/boards-and-commissions.html	(307) 777-5647

Appendix D - State Workers' Compensation Divisions

State	Main Website	Workers' Compensation Website	Phone Number
Alabama	www.alabama.gov	http://dir.alabama.gov/wc/	334-353-0690
Alaska	www.state.ak.us	http://www.labor.state.ak.us/wc/wc.htm	(907) 465-2790
Arizona	www.az.gov	http://www.ica.state.az.us/workersCompensation/index.html	(602) 542-4653
Arkansas	www.state.ar.us	http://www.awcc.state.ar.us/	(501)682-3930
California	www.ca.gov	http://www.dir.ca.gov/dwc/dwc_home_page.htm	(800) 736-7401
Colorado	www.colorado.gov	http://www.coworkforce.com/DWC/	(303) 318-8700
Connecticut	www.ct.gov	http://wcc.state.ct.us/	(860) 493-1500
Delaware	www.delaware.gov	http://www.delawareworks.com/industrialaffairs/services/workerscomp.shtml	(302)761-8200
District of Columbia	http://www.dc.gov/	http://www.does.dc.gov/does/cwp/view.asp?a=1232&Q=537428	(202) 671-1000
Florida	www.myflorida.com	http://www.fldfs.com/WC/	(850) 413-1601
Georgia	www.georgia.gov	http://sbwc.georgia.gov/02/sbwc/home/0,2235,11394008,00.html	404-656-2048
Hawaii	www.ehawaii.gov	http://hawaii.gov/labor/dcd/aboutwc.shtml	(808) 586-9166
Idaho	www.idaho.gov	www.icc.idaho.gov	208-334-6000
Illinois	www.illinois.gov	http://www.iic.idaho.gov/	208-334-6000
Indiana	www.in.gov	http://www.in.gov/workcomp/	(317)232-3809
Iowa	www.iowa.gov	http://www.iowaworkforce.org/wc/	(515) 281-5387
Kansas	www.kansas.gov	http://www.dol.ks.gov/WC/html/wc_ALL.html	(785) 296-6762
Kentucky	www.kentucky.gov	http://labor.ky.gov/workersclaims/	(502) 564-5550
Louisiana	www.louisiana.gov	http://www.laworks.net/WorkersComp/OWC_Worker-Menu.asp	(225)342-3111
Maine	www.maine.gov	http://www.state.me.us/wcb/	(207) 287-3751

State	Main Website	Workers' Compensation Website	Phone Number
Maryland	www.maryland.gov	http://www.wcc.state.md.us/	(410)864-5100
Massachusetts	www.state.ma.us	http://www.state.ma.us/wcac/wcac.html	(617) 727-4900
Michigan	www.michigan.gov	http://www.michigan.gov/wca	(888)396-5041
Minnesota	www.state.mn.us	http://www.oah.state.mn.us/wc.html	(651) 361-7863
Mississippi	www.mississippi.gov	http://www.mwcc.state.ms.us/	(866) 473-6922
Missouri	www.missouri.gov	http://www.dolir.mo.gov/wc/	(573) 751-4231
Montana	www.mt.gov	http://wcc.dli.state.mt.us/	(406) 444-7794
Nebraska	www.state.ne.us	http://www.nol.org/home/WC/	(402) 471 6455
Nevada	www.nv.gov	http://dirweb.state.nv.us/WCS/wcs.htm	(775) 684-7260
New Hampshire	www.nh.gov	http://www.labor.state.nh.us/	(603) 271-3176
New Jersey	www.nj.gov	http://lwd.dol.state.nj.us/labor/wc/wc_index.html	(609) 292 2515
New Mexico	www.newmexico.gov	http://www.workerscomp.state.nm.us/	(505)841-6000
New York	www.state.ny.us	http://www.wcb.state.ny.us/	(877) 632-4996
N. Carolina	www.ncgov.com	www.ic.nc.gov	(800) 688 8349
N. Dakota	www.nd.gov	http://www.WorkforceSafety.com/	(800) 777-5033
Ohio	www.ohio.gov	http://www.ohiobwc.com/	(800) 644-6292
Oklahoma	www.ok.gov	http://www.owcc.state.ok.us/	(405) 522-8600
Oregon	www.oregon.gov	http://wcd.oregon.gov/	(800)452 0288
Pennsylvania	www.state.pa.us	http://www.dli.state.pa.us/landi/cwp/view.asp?a=138&q=220671	(717)772-4447
Rhode Island	www.ri.gov	http://www.dlt.ri.gov/wc/	(401) 462-8100
S. Carolina	www.sc.gov	http://www.wcc.state.sc.us/	(803)737-5700
S.Dakota	www.state.sd.us	http://dol.sd.gov/workerscomp/default.aspx	(605)773-3681
Tennessee	www.state.tn.us	http://www.state.tn.us/labor-wfd/wcomp.html	(615)532-4812
Texas	www.tx.us	http://www.tdi.state.tx.us/wc/indexwc.html	(888)489-2667
Utah	www.utah.gov	http://www.laborcommission.utah.gov/IndustrialAccidents/index.html	(801) 530-6800
Vermont	www.vermont.gov	http://www.labor.vermont.gov/	(802)828-4000
Virginia	www.virginia.gov	http://www.vwc.state.va.us	(877) 664-2566
Washington	www.access.wa.gov	http://www.lni.wa.gov/	(800) 647-0982
W.Virginia	www.wv.gov	http://www.wvinsurance.gov/	(304) 558-3386
Wisconsin	www.wisconsin.gov	http://www.dwd.state.wi.us/wc/default.htm	(608) 266-1340
Wyoming	www.wyoming.gov	http://wydoe.state.wy.us/doe.asp?ID=9	(307) 777-5476

Appendix E - State Divisions of Corporations

State	Main Website	Corporation Search	Phone Number
Alabama	www.alabama.gov	http://www.sos.alabama.gov/vb/inquiry/inquiry.aspx?area=Corporations	334-242-5324
Alaska	www.state.ak.us	https://myalaska.state.ak.us/business/soskb/CSearch.asp	(907) 465-5211

State	Main Website	Corporation Search	Phone Number
Arizona	www.az.gov	http://starpas.azcc.gov/scripts/cgiip.exe/WService=wsbroker1/main.p	602-542-3026
Arkansas	www.state.ar.us	http://www.sos.arkansas.gov/corps/index.html	(501) 682-1010
California	www.ca.gov	http://kepler.sos.ca.gov/list.html	(916) 657-5448
Colorado	www.colorado.gov	http://www.sos.state.co.us/biz/BusinessEntityCriteriaExt.do?resetTransTyp=Y	(303) 894 2200 ext.2
Connecticut	www.ct.gov	http://www.concord-sots.ct.gov/CONCORD/online?sn=InquiryServlet&eid=99	(860) 509-6002
Delaware	www.delaware.gov	https://sos-res.state.de.us/tin/GINameSearch.jsp	(302) 739-3073
D.C.	www.dc.gov	http://lsdbe.dslbd.dc.gov/public/certification/search.aspx?olbdNav=I31105I	(202) 727-3900
Florida	www.myflorida.com	http://www.sunbiz.org/search.html	(850) 245-6052
Georgia	www.georgia.gov	http://corp.sos.state.ga.us/corp/soskb/csearch.asp	404.656.2817
Hawaii	www.ehawaii.gov	http://hbe.ehawaii.gov/documents/search.html	(808) 586-2727
Idaho	www.idaho.gov	http://www.accessidaho.org/public/sos/corp/search.html	(208) 334-2300
Illinois	www.illinois.gov	http://www.cyberdriveillinois.com/departments/business_services/corp.html	(217) 782-6961
Indiana	www.in.gov	http://www.in.gov/sos/business/corps/searches.html	(317) 232-6531
Iowa	www.iowa.gov	http://www.iowalifechanging.com/business/blic.aspx	(800) 532-1216
Kansas	www.kansas.gov	http://www.accesskansas.org/srv-corporations/search.do	(225) 925-4704
Kentucky	www.kentucky.gov	http://www.sos.ky.gov/business/online/	(502) 564-3490
Louisiana	www.louisiana.gov	http://www400.sos.louisiana.gov/app1/paygate/crpinq.jsp	(225) 925-4704
Maine	www.maine.gov	http://icrs.informe.org/nei-sos-icrs/ICRS	(207) 624-7736
Maryland	www.maryland.gov	http://www.blis.state.md.us/	888-ChooseMD
Massachusetts	www.state.ma.us	http://corp.sec.state.ma.us/corp/corpsearch/corpsearchinput.asp	(617) 727-9640
Minnesota	www.state.mn.us	http://da.sos.state.mn.us/minnesota/corp_inquiry-find.asp?:Norder_item_type_id=10&sm=7	(651) 297-7067
Mississippi	www.mississippi.gov	https://business.sos.state.ms.us/corp/soskb/csearch.asp	(601) 359-1350
Missouri	www.missouri.gov	https://www.sos.mo.gov/BusinessEntity/soskb/csearch.asp	(573) 751-4153
Montana	www.mt.gov	http://app.mt.gov/bes/	(404) 444-3665
Nebraska	www.nebraska.gov	https://www.nebraska.gov/sos/corp/corpsearch.cgi?nav=search	1-800-747-8177
Nevada	www.nv.gov	https://esos.state.nv.us/SOSServices/AnonymousAccess/CorpSearch/CorpSearch.aspx	(775) 684-5708
New Hampshire	www.nh.gov	https://www.sos.nh.gov/corporate/soskb/csearch.asp	(603) 271-3246
New Jersey	www.nj.gov	https://accessnet.state.nj.us/home.asp	(609) 292-9292
New Mexico	www.newmexico.gov	http://www.nmprc.state.nm.us/cii.htm	(505) 827-4508
New York	www.state.ny.us	http://appsext8.dos.state.ny.us/corp_public/CORP-SEARCH.ENTITY_SEARCH_ENTRY	(518) 473-2492
N. Carolina	www.ncgov.com	http://www.secretary.state.nc.us/corporations/CSearch.aspx	(919) 807-2000
N. Dakota	www.nd.gov	https://secure.apps.state.nd.us/sc/busnsrch/busnSearch.htm	(701) 328-4284
Ohio	www.ohio.gov	http://www2.sos.state.oh.us/portal/page?_pageid=35,58664,35_58678&_dad=portal&_schema=PORTAL	1-877-SOS-FILE

State	Main Website	Corporation Search	Phone Number
Oklahoma	www.ok.gov	http://www.ok.gov/redirect.php?link_id=472	(405) 521-3912
Oregon	www.oregon.gov	http://egov.sos.state.or.us/br/pkg_web_name_srch_inq. login	(503) 986 2200
Pennsylvania	www.state.pa.us	https://www.corporations.state.pa.us/corp/soskb/csearch. asp	(717) 787-1057
Rhode Island	www.ri.gov	http://www.riedc.com/data-and-publications/find-a-business	401-278-9100 ext. 122
S. Carolina	www.sc.gov	http://www.scsos.com/Search%20Business%20Filings	(803) 734-2158
S. Dakota	www.state.sd.us	http://apps.sd.gov/applications/st32cprs/soscorplookup. aspx	(605) 773-4845
Tennessee	www.state.tn.us	http://www.tennesseeanytime.org/soscorp/	(615) 741-2286
Texas	www.texas.gov	http://ecpa.cpa.state.tx.us/coa/Index.html	1-800-252-1386
Utah	www.utah.gov	https://secure.utah.gov/bes/action/index	(801) 530-4849
Vermont	www.vermont.gov	http://www.sec.state.vt.us/seek/corpbrow.htm	(802) 828-2386
Virginia	www.virginia.gov	http://s0302.vita.virginia.gov/servlet/resqportal/ resqportal?&rqs_custom_dir=scccisp1	(804) 371-9733
Washington	www.access.wa.gov	http://www.secstate.wa.gov/corps/corps_search.aspx	360-725-0377.
W. Virginia	www.wv.gov	http://www.wvsos.com/wvcorporations/verifylogon.asp	(304) 558-8000
Wisconsin	www.wisconsin.gov	http://www.wdfi.org/apps/CorpSearch/Search.aspx?	(608) 261-7577
Wyoming	www.wyoming.gov	https://wyobiz.wy.gov/Ecommerce/SearchResultNew.aspx	(307) 777-7311

INDEX

C

Additional Thanks

Kim Niv – Florida Surety Bonds
David Burr – Insurance Office of America
Michelle Delaney – The Page Insurance Company
Dennis Ragsdale – City of St. Cloud
Cynthia Skogsberg – Post, Buckley, Schuh and Jernigan
Ann Hagen – Bonded Builders Warranty Group
Kim Griffin – Arlington Homes
Jon Clarke – Jacks and Sticks
Ron MacDonald – RAM Graphics
Tobias Franoszek – Concept Miami

…and to the editors who help me build a sound book.

If you found this book to be informative and helpful, please spread the word on:
• Facebook, Twitter, and other social networking websites
• Amazon.com
• Blogs and email
• And good ol' fashioned word of mouth

Comments are welcome at www.thecontractress.com